BEING HERE NOW

Ganesh N Rajan

Copyright © Ganesh Natarajan 2022
All Rights Reserved.

ISBN 979-8-88805-527-4

This book has been published with all efforts taken to make the material error-free after the consent of the author. However, the author and the publisher do not assume and hereby disclaim any liability to any party for any loss, damage, or disruption caused by errors or omissions, whether such errors or omissions result from negligence, accident, or any other cause.

While every effort has been made to avoid any mistake or omission, this publication is being sold on the condition and understanding that neither the author nor the publishers or printers would be liable in any manner to any person by reason of any mistake or omission in this publication or for any action taken or omitted to be taken or advice rendered or accepted on the basis of this work. For any defect in printing or binding the publishers will be liable only to replace the defective copy by another copy of this work then available.

TABLE OF CONTENTS

PART I: The Problem

PART II: The Preparation

PART V: The Conclusion

PRAISE FOR THE FIRST EDITION

(First published as "I, Me, and Us")

I have read many first-person accounts of the experiences that people have gone through when they've been afflicted by the most devastating of psychiatric disorders—Schizophrenia. But, in all truth, I've never read one like *I, ME and US*. What makes it so special are the insights that Ganesh, the author, has not merely obtained but also shared with such lucidity to anyone who reads this wonderful book. What's most interesting is that the insights are not limited merely to surviving the illness but have to do with life and the cognitive experience itself. Well structured, crisp and clear, the book can help anyone looking for a roadmap to maneuver their way around the speed bumps and potholes that our lives today encounter. It's a terrific read and one that I would recommend to all those who are looking for some anchor points with which to navigate life's vagaries.'

– Dr. Vijay Nagaswami:
Psychiatrist and Bestselling Author

'*I, ME and US* is written by a person who has had to contend with a major psychiatric disorder in the best years of his life and yet has managed to lead a meaningful existence with a good work record, a family, and a zest to share his life experiences. This book epitomizes the fact that persons with major mental disorders can attain a state of normality comparable to others. This is well in keeping with the concept of recovery that is being targeted all over the world as a desirable outcome. While those with schizophrenia and their family members will probably identify with the experiences recounted in the narrative, this isn't all the book has to offer. As the author himself mentions, he has spoken of philosophy, psychology, and self-help. You will therefore find tips to cope with mental illness interlaced with philosophical and existential themes in a very intriguing and interesting manner.'

– Dr. R Thara, Director: Schizophrenia
Research Foundation (SCARF), Chennai, India.

'Schizophrenia is one of the most devastating mental illnesses anyone can encounter. Suffering from this disorder and coming to terms with it, gaining insight into the illness, continuing medication, and ultimately triumphing over this malady is not something easy to achieve. Ganesh Rajan has achieved this rather difficult feat with great aplomb... This book is in the form of a narrative about the illness, the process, and recovery, with an emphasis on adherence to medication, while it also has a lot of self-analyses by the author. This narration will surely help on how to cope with this problem... He has written this volume under various chapters with a liberal sprinkling of supporting insights from diverse sources. It speaks volumes of his erudition and depth of knowledge, not only in what he is trying to convey but also his knowledge in the field of literature.'

– Dr S. Kalyanasundaram, Hon.
CEO: Richmond Fellowship Society &
Professor of Psychiatry and Principal:
RF PG College for Psychosocial Rehabilitation, Bengaluru, India

PREFACE TO THE SECOND EDITION

Time has humbled, wizened, and made me better with what I want to share. As a result, I think this second edition is easier to read and understand than its first attempt.

I harbored doubts; how could I help when *I* needed help? How do I include others as part of my life's purpose? Finally, I decided to plow ahead because I enjoyed writing and refining. But surprising serendipity followed.

I experienced growth exceeding expectations as I articulated the ideas in the book. My experience in taking what life can dish out, my ability to be proactive, and my capacity to be patient grew significantly. However, like before, I feel the true example of its lessons is a person I have only glimpsed in my mind's eye. That person will love what he does and enjoy life to the fullest possible.

I hope to help you, albeit obliquely, discover your personal purpose and what you love doing. Doing what you love to do will make many doubts vanish. The questions will drop off.

Quite a few of the referenced footnotes from the first edition may seem ancient, but that doesn't change their truths. It has been said, "All wisdom is plagiarism. Only stupidity is original." The wisdom thinkers have shared, therefore, does not fade away.

I hope you enjoy reading it as much as I loved writing this new edition. I wish you wellness... always, Ganesh, Sep 2022.

PREFACE TO THE FIRST EDITION

[For convenience, the first published title has been replaced]

What are the shareable insights an ex-schizophrenic can have? As a person with schizophrenia, I felt unequipped to face life. I woke up to a world playing various games loaded with discouraging psychosocial measures and rules. Even ordinary people appeared to me as wrestling ineffectively with their situation.

Some had severe hang-ups from the past. Others constantly compared their lot with those around them. Yet others read a deceptively supernatural twist in their reality.

Going through schizophrenia opened my eyes to the importance of having a practical and real personal purpose. Several insights helped me be more proactive, confident, and poised. I feel the revelations I stumbled upon, and built on, are too valuable to keep confined to myself.

Why aren't there books that can reassure and teach us that one can succeed without having to be the best of the best? Why are people measuring their success in comparison with others? Why do environmental cues promote such relative successes? What makes some of us succumb to superstition and the surreal in thought, word, and deed? Where are the answers for the millions who live modestly, going from challenge to challenge, just living?

As a response to such questions, I have tried to explore a broad, all-encompassing goal: How can anyone genuinely belong in life?

This book attempts to do justice to this broad and ambitious intent despite my limitations.

BEING HERE NOW uses schizophrenia to explore many kinds of negativity both for the sane and the obviously afflicted. The book has a generous dose of prescriptive and generic advice. I explore some ideas and techniques that can help us recognize our own uniqueness and become proactive in our approach. I go over Creation, interaction, and gumption from fresh perspectives.

I think I have thrown in everything but the kitchen sink into the book to be comprehensive. A kitchen sink in context, which you may notice as missing, are explanations for pointless pain: Pain and suffering that is neither an alarm nor a teacher or part of an addressable mission. Such issues, I am saving to ask of the Big One!

* * *

Schizophrenia is a much-misunderstood condition. According to statistics, schizophrenia affects 1 percent of the population (at some point in life). This condition is independent of nationality, social or economic status, religion, and gender. Most people confuse it with multiple personality disorder, but schizophrenia is different. Schizophrenia is a mental manifestation of a physical condition.

The symptoms of schizophrenia are of two kinds—positive and negative. The positive symptoms refer to signs that should not be present but are, such as delusions and hallucinations. A delusion is a false, fixed belief. Persons with schizophrenia hold on to it with such conviction that logical reasoning or evidence to the contrary cannot shake it. A hallucination is a sensory perception without stimulus. Hallucinations may be auditory, visual, tactile, or olfactory.

Negative symptoms of schizophrenia are called such because they are related to normal behaviors absent in afflicted persons. These symptoms reflect the loss or absence of standard traits or abilities. Common negative symptoms are flat or blunted emotion, poverty of speech, inability to experience pleasure, lack of desire to form relationships, and lack of motivation.

While medication can alleviate the positive symptoms of schizophrenia, the negative symptoms often remain. This could prevent persons with schizophrenia from getting back into the social mainstream.

Dr. RD Laing (1927–87) was a noted British psychiatrist known for his out-of-the-box thinking. He blamed society's unliveable condition for the rise of schizophrenia and other mental illnesses. Marshall McLuhan (1911–80), a prominent Canadian communications theorist, suggested, 'Schizophrenia may be a necessary consequence (sic) of literacy.' Some claim 'stress-diathesis,' a combination of stress and dormant triggers, causes the illness.

I agree with the theories that suggest the reasons for the onset are psychological or psychosocial and not just physiological. I hence feel that empathizing with the afflicted person and applying tactful nudges towards reality can prevent aggravation or bring about enduring remission. With willingness and a push towards normality, many can achieve a sense of wellness and return to mainstream social life.

* * *

A fictional dialogue with a young person having schizophrenia precedes all chapters, save the last one. This preamble to each chapter is entirely fabricated, and primarily a device introduced to thread the book's concepts.

I portray the person with schizophrenia as articulate, despite his illness. Furthermore, the maverick therapeutic approach and rapid recovery depicted are atypical. I have written with a great extent of literary license so that it can be relevant to a diverse and broad audience.

I must also apologize upfront for playing fast and loose with the terms schizophrenic, affliction, disability, patient, and the like, using the same license. Many are still trying to sort out the stigma and negative connotations of such terms. I want to add to mental illness awareness and understanding and prevent the onset, not compound any confusion.

BEING HERE NOW is an eclectic combination of philosophy, psychology, and self-help. It is, in some ways, an attempt to define what is sane and what is successful. We know sanity and success, but they elude a straitjacket definition.

Regardless of who you are, you will hopefully discover a sense of success, sanity, and wellness by considering the book's concepts. While it is hard to be generic and still address individual problems, *BEING HERE NOW*, I believe, has enough information to help everybody. Therefore, don't think I don't have schizophrenia, so this is not for me.

I have used the pronoun 'He' throughout the work for convenience. Still, schizophrenia does not discriminate, and the references are equally applicable to all genders.

I hope that *BEING HERE NOW* will help demystify life and make our world better. If some explanations in the book seem radical, just enjoy the irreverence. Don't shoot the messenger! My goal is to be helpful to the greatest number, to the most significant degree. Read on!

– Ganesh N. Rajan
February 2015.
Enhanced September 2022,
India

BEING HERE NOW
Insights of an ex-schizophrenic

PART I: The Problem

I put together the following anecdote based on an illustration shared in a publication for children. A long time ago, a missionary in Africa sent a native to another mission in a neighboring village to borrow a hammer. The preacher made the native wear a wooden plaque around his neck. It had the words, 'SEND HAMMER' burnt into the wood. The native went to the neighboring village, was given the hammer at the mission, and returned with it. The native was convinced the spell carved on the plaque had made spirits talk and ask for the hammer. The missionary explained that no ghosts had talked and that the spell was written language. The native answered, 'If it talks without speaking, it is a spirit.'

CHAPTER 1

INTROSPECTION

The parents seemed unsure of where to start. Dr. Dharmaraj, the psychiatrist, opened the discussion by asking broad questions about the family to put them at ease. Then, when he asked if there had been any out-of-the-ordinary behavior, it was like turning on a tap.

Nachiket was a nineteen-year-old boy. He was under a delusion that he was the mythical Nachiketa reborn. The doctor knew the Hindu mythological tale. A father makes an offering of his son, Nachiketa, to Yama, the God of death and justice.

The mythical Nachiketa's father, Vaajasravas, was a rigorous practitioner of Hindu rituals. He performed a *yagna*[1], as part of which he gave away cows in ritualistic compensation. However, these cows found it difficult to even eat grass or drink water, let alone yield milk! They were too old to be put to any use.

Seeing this, his virtuous and intelligent son, Nachiketa, foresaw great sorrow for his father because of the flawed offerings. Nachiketa wanted to save Vaajasravas from this fate. To shock his father into seeing sense, the boy asked to whom he intended to offer his own son as a gift. He pestered Vaajasravas to give him away to someone as well.

At this, Vaajasravas got so annoyed that he declared in disgust, 'I am giving you to the God of Death.' Nachiketa then resolved that he must make his father's words come true, though they were uttered in anger.

---

1   An event of communal offering in the Hindu religion

So, the boy persuaded his father to offer him as a gift to Yama, the God of Death, in a strict ritualistic style.

The story goes that, impressed by Nachiketa's fearlessness, Yama gave him three boons. Then, as one boon, Nachiketa asked for the ability to understand if a mortal exists after death and how. The ensuing dialogue between Yama and Nachiketa, prompted by this question, is the focus of the Hindu scripture known as the *Kathopanishad*.

Our fictional patient, the delusional Nachiket, was a quiet person. He had been furiously reading various scriptures and philosophical texts for the past six weeks, ignoring everything else. He hadn't slept or eaten much in the past two weeks and was answering all questions in monosyllables. The past two nights, he had just kept awake. Now he refused to speak, communicating only with a nod or shaking his head.

He had stalled all attempts by his parents to take him to a doctor. The only reason he agreed now seemed to be that the doctor's name was Dharmaraj. Dharmaraj is another name for Yama in his role as the dispenser of ultimate justice.

Nachiket's parents had built up on the doctor's name to lure the boy into a meeting, even implying the doctor's divinity. The parents pleaded with the doctor that if he went along with their son's delusion, Dharmaraj could persuade the youth to talk. The depth of this delusion was so immense that to do otherwise seemed a dead end.

The doctor asked the parents to send in Nachiket, who was sitting outside in the waiting area. He entered the doctor's chamber unaccompanied. The boy's eyes were wild, but he seemed sure of himself and willingly started to talk. A few seconds into the conversation, the doctor realized that this role-play would be more taxing than anticipated.

'You are Dharmaraj, right?' Nachiket asked.

'Yes,' the doctor replied, glad that Nachiket had framed his question so that he did not have to lie.

'So, you must know why I am here,' Nachiket continued.

'Yes, I do, but I would like to hear it from you,' the doctor said, still hedging.

Nachiket spoke excitedly, taking for granted that Dharmaraj was divine, 'First, I thank you, Lord of Dharma, for all you shared with me of the afterlife. I still have some questions, not about the afterlife, but about life itself. How can I understand you, and how will I carry this understanding forward?'

The doctor took a deep breath before answering, pondering the ethical implications of continuing in this manner. 'You understand me because we were created to understand each other. The human species alone, in all of Creation, has the gift of language and the ability to communicate complex spoken and written notions. Language enables us to understand each other and carry the understanding forward.'

Nachiket continued, 'Does this mean I can convey to another, as lucidly as you have conveyed to me, the subjects we have explored?'

Dharmaraj decided to get into the role as earnestly as possible. It would be a breakthrough if he could guide Nachiket out of his delusion, even if it was an unorthodox approach.

'Soon, humanity will have instruments that make it possible to reproduce accurately any communication by another human. Moreover, these future instruments will be able to record interactions in a manner unknown today. They will capture every word, every inflection, and visible action humans perform in glorious three-dimensionality. This will certainly enhance communication.'

'That is so wonderful!' exclaimed Nachiket. 'This means every human will understand exactly the way I have, as I will be able to reproduce my experience and understanding exactly. I hear voices, see symbols, and smell things that no one else can. I believe you have granted me these powers for a purpose.'

Dharmaraj attempted to gently introduce a real focus. 'Each of us sees and understands creation based on personal experience. At the core of understanding is a unique self, qualifying all stimulation one receives. The understanding could be helpful or flawed.'

Nachiket went on with his questions, 'What decides how each person understands something, independent of the message? Is it the message or our understanding of it that is flawed?'

Dharmaraj then spoke about the learning of the human species. 'We are independent conscious beings in some respects and connected to the species in others. This connectivity extends a person's learning beyond specific individual experiences. What one understands depends on a collective learning of the species and the individual's independent learning. Both kinds of learning may be helpful or flawed and subtle or self-evident.'

Nachiket was full of questions. He continued, 'Will we ever know what is damaging our understanding so we can take corrective action?'

Dharmaraj answered, 'Some of this is sewn into your very being and can only be experienced. It comes to you as a disposition — learning that you have no control over. It exists as much as we exist as a species. The good news is any damaging impact can be managed with effort and a personal willingness to change.'

'Do I have this learning of my species in me?' Nachiket asked.

Dharmaraj tried to describe the species' learning as he confirmed Nachiket's query. 'Surely, you do. A part of the learning is mechanical, but a part of it is moderated through the unique ability we have as a human species—that of language. This brings us back to your earlier question: How do you understand my ideas and me?

I must answer there are two influencers. One is your conscious recognition of patterns, such as language—over which you have some control. And two, an inner witness deciding your reaction to the patterns—over which you may have limited or no control.'

Nachiket was keen to know more. 'Is there a common way the inner witness reacts for all of us?'

The doctor chose his words carefully. 'You have some mental repositories in which some patterns become residual. Our background and experience imprint these residual patterns long before we attain the capability to judge them as right or wrong.

These include impressions of forces like culture, local adaptations, tradition, language, and race. These impressions guide us before we get the ability to decide independently.

You could become aware of such repositories when you are a child, a youth, or an older person. At this point, we would also see our situation as woeful or favorable. One can see oneself as an evolving being from the moment we awake to our reality, or adversely, as thrown into the vicissitudes of living. So, let me ask you—do you feel awake or asleep, disadvantaged or in control?'

Nachiket provided another clue on his mental state and paranoid condition, 'I feel others can read my mind and are hiding a different knowledge from me. Therefore, I came to you.

'Can you write what you feel and bring it to me?' The doctor asked, knowing that keeping a journal, though difficult, would help Nachiket focus.

'I will try to do that,' Nachiket answered. 'So many ideas and voices crowd my head.'

'Let us meet again... Okay?' The doctor concluded. 'I am prescribing some pills for you to take in the meantime. These should help you with clearing up your head.'

'I will take it as *prasad*[2],' said Nachiket reverently.

Dr. Dharmaraj called in the parents while Nachiket sat outside. The doctor shared his preliminary diagnosis of schizophrenia and explained the condition. He also explained that recovery might take a while, as it usually needs a few trials to get the medication right, if at all. In addition, different people need different combinations with varying dosage levels.

Medication is often lifelong but sometimes is needed only for a short while. For the time being, the doctor recommended that the parents avoid confronting Nachiket or pander to his delusions. The doctor was happy that Nachiket did not refuse medication.

THE COMMON CONFUSION

Section Highlights:

- A sense of inadequacy is behind a wide range of damaging thoughts for both the afflicted and normal.
- Persons with schizophrenia lack explanations for the symptoms they experience and may hence adopt spurious reasoning.
- We can derive lessons from schizophrenic experiences and overcome much of our unproductive thinking.
- Any aberrations can be nullified by understanding the four problems of misplaced theory, incorrect symbolic cues, misdirected social pressures, and the trauma of human birth.

The human species is at the pinnacle of the evolutionary pyramid. Yet, many are adrift in this world. Some people do experience odd happenings that conflict with rational thought. Nachiket was one such individual. He found himself in a contorted reality that begged new explanations.

---

2   Blessed and holy food in Hinduism

Professionals classify the experiences of a person with schizophrenia, such as hallucinations and delusions, as only superficial symptoms of a deeper physical malaise. These symptoms, however, appear tangible and authentic to the experiencer. The individual thus faces a perplexing *personal* reality. It demands a new approach from all that the person has learned.

He could try to force-fit, unsuccessfully, the oddities he perceives using only the knowledge he presently has. Because he lacks explanations, an afflicted person may imaginatively link up trivia. He could overlay spurious meanings onto the inane. The behavior resulting from such attempts will seem bizarre to a 'normal' observer.

In the commonly understood measures of normality, ordinary people also experience obscure dark phases. This 'darkness' occurs when they have insufficient knowledge to handle what they face, as in afflicted people.

When faced with an unfamiliar environment, a special relationship, or a different philosophy, an average person could also slip into a milder form of unhelpful thinking. For some, new paradigms may trigger timidity, fear, anxiety, and other negatives. A shortfall in learning may almost force some people to be irrational, unreasonable, or aggressive in their attempts to strike a balance.

Since reality is, in several ways, different from whatever theory can explain, some people may gradually descend into negative thinking.

Schizophrenia is likely to emerge from a 'limiting ideology' adopted early in life rather than when keeping an open mind. Limiting ideologies are introverted beliefs primarily influenced by the past. They keep a person in a comfortable, seemingly normal, but artificial cocoon. Such limiting doctrines, typically, are not in touch with practical realities.

When stress triggers a strange sensitivity, the person could perceive an inexplicable private reality. With growing distress, an invasive environment never ever felt before could be experienced by the individual. An overly sensitive regular individual could retreat psychologically and become diffident or aggressive. Some would have the onset of a mental disability like schizophrenia.

Why are some people more sensitive than others? What are the forces that turn a sensible child into an insecure adult? What made Nachiket look to mythology for answers? How can the experiences of a person who went through schizophrenia help ordinary people? Where is the parallel with schizophrenia? The similarity may be a lack of critical foundational knowledge in persons with schizophrenia and other ordinary people.

In both afflicted and normal individuals, the learning acquired thus far by the person is unable to explain a new experience. A feeling of being inadequate can cause reactive or unreasonable behavior in anyone. This is the 'common confusion' in both the afflicted and normal.

Going forward into the book, the fictional Dr. Dharmaraj implies four problems hold us back from functioning well. Firstly, flawed showcasing of competition and winning. Secondly, faulty corporal, linguistic, or other symbolic cues, including the so-called hallucinations and surreal derivations. Thirdly, social pressures that foster what we argue are misplaced desires to be superior. Finally, the trauma of being born is our fourth problem.

Human birth might be the most harrowing original traumatic experience an individual undergoes. The change in environment from the womb to the outside world is shocking. This birthing trauma is likely to have influenced our early actions and experiences, some of which could have been harmful.

Explanations for these problems, and advice on coping with them, could help you be more poised, proactive, and productive. It worked for me as the book evolved.

You are reading this book after making a conscious decision to do it. You read this and make sense of the words you are reading. This is impossible for any other primate. But, then again, is the human species all that special? Many still carry out uncivilized and barbaric acts. *Can anyone genuinely validate that we are a civilized society? Can any one person tell others how they should be?*

This book ambitiously asserts that there are explanations for *all that is* in creation. It is emphatic in claiming that we can resolve many factors that cause adverse feelings. The book should help you overcome many oppressive elements and much inner conflict. It would also help alleviate feelings of being a victim in an unfair, unjust environment.

Those who find a deeper purpose can feel and make a difference. Give yourself a chance to accept being (in the) here (and the) now. Be willing. The rest is easy.

SUFFERING SYMBOLISM

Section Highlights

- Humans could be the only species possessing the trait of advanced symbolism and language.
- Our theoretical repository is often confusing and contradictory because it is an inadequate tool to capture the practical accurately.
- A literate person tends to imbibe conflicting theories without forming his unique worldview.
- The prime theoretical belief handed down and accepted popularly is the need to compete, win and be one-up on others.
- The need to compete, win and be one-up on others may be from a distortion of the concept of natural selection and a misdirected societal nurture.
- Our social structures ostensibly uphold parity, fair opportunity, and recognition of merit. Still, many norms seem biased.
- Understanding why and how we are conditioned by collective influences can prevent us from slipping into (or recovering from) damaging thoughts.

Consider that schizophrenia may be a consequence of literacy—an observation made by Marshall McLuhan (1911–80), a prominent Canadian communications theorist. To set the context, we can ask: *What is the genesis of literacy? How did we humans become literate in the first place, flaws and all?* To answer, I'll briefly indulge in pop-Darwinism.

There is a hypothesis that the division of the human brain into right and left hemispheres could be a result of evolution. The idea suggests that humans gradually mutated to have this division as a backup. Our species, helped by such a backup, could have survived cranial damage from events such as falling rocks or the jaws of a predator[3].

Subsequently, this 'spare' brain enabled specialization within each hemisphere. Unlike other species with dual hemispherical brains, this backup lent itself to something more for us humans. Its size, neuron density, and the availability of abundant energy from easily digestible cooked food enabled this.

Cooking allowed us to ingest many calories in a much shorter time than other species that ate only a little by little and over a long time. Therefore, the discovery of cooking left us sufficient time to carry out other activities and for our intellect to develop[4].

According to the theory of evolution, whenever a minor change in a being's physiology aids its survival, this change is emphasized. This continues until it is full-blown or until it loses its importance as a survival tool.

The human right-brain developed the ability to understand relationships in space and time. The left-brain became responsible for fine physical manipulations and *language*.

---

3   Joel Achenbach: Why Things Are: Answers to Every Essential Question in Life; New York: Ballantine Books; 1991

4   This is a novel idea proposed by Suzana Herculano-Houzel, an associate professor at the Federal University of Rio de Janeiro, Brazil.

Whatever the genesis, literacy, language, and associated symbolic representations are here to stay with us. We seem to be the only ones privileged to transmit words, phrases, or even scientific formulae, using multiple mediums. Symbolic representation, such as language, which can communicate across more than one physical sense, is a quality owned by humans alone.

Dogs, dolphins, and honeybees lack the alphabet, Braille, or a national constitution. Only humans can share ideas through speech, sight, and touch. A language transmitted across the senses, and on this scale, is absent in any other living thing, perhaps even in the entire cosmos. There is no proof to this date otherwise.

As of now, we are the sole literates of the Universe. Nevertheless, this power could be a dubious distinction. These human powers are mostly a blessing, but sometimes they are misapplied.

Consider that this information age affects the literate and educated more than the less read. We, the literate, encounter volumes of information. This information can be constructive as well as destructive. Words are only tools; therefore, people can use them for good and bad. Tomes, such as national constitutions, and Hitler's *Mein Kampf,* are all part of this collection of information.

Different versions, new facts, and news are constantly pounding the literate. A metropolis would have many newspapers. An adult literate person like Nachiket would have read the works of several authors. Different media expose the individual to various ideologies. Views on reality and ideas in worlds of fiction influence our thinking.

We have ideas that contradict each other and ideas that seem correct but become incorrect later. Ideas in politics, the sciences, the humanities, and the arts keep changing. One may have accepted a lot of information from diverse sources as plausible simply because there are no alternative explanations.

When scientists declare that lifeforms today result from 'natural selection' or economists say that the market is driven by 'competition,' or when gurus proclaim that 'self-enlightenment' is our goal, people accept these as accurate.

To help cope while growing up, many of us absorb half-truths and justifications - we accept some 'facts' handed down by family and friends without question. This could range from distorted religion to homespun wisdom.

We read books or listen to proclaimed experts in ideologies when we need advice. Often, this information is incomplete and susceptible to challenge as we mature. As a result, some of us keep questioning our situation. We ask, *'Why me?'* or *'Why this?'*, despite umpteen attempts to explain and rationalize all we face.

As thinking beings, we seek complete explanations. We like to believe that what we sense in our reality is wholly true and can be validated. But, unfortunately, quite a few of us miss the fine print that our lives may never be verifiably complete, entirely truthful, or always just.

For instance, theoretical economics suggests that markets can ensure the best will succeed using supply and demand to sift through mediocrity. But, in fact, society may fail to reward the deserving in many cases. Don't we already know from news or experience that the norms of truth and justice are sometimes transgressed?

* * *

Our predecessors have handed down many assorted theories, some as old as the advent of language itself. Yet, despite its age, most of our theoretical knowledge has evolved in isolated pockets of understanding. This is because of geographical remoteness between early human settlements, language barriers, and the continuing tendency of knowledge streams to specialize.

Our theory also seems inadequate because of practical limits in expression using any language. No existing ideology, including the idea that merit is rewarded, appears complete. Therefore, several doctrines containing leftovers from yesterday perpetuate conflict.

The fact that religions continue to engage in one-upmanship is testimony to the confusion caused by the written word. No ideology, it appears, can offer convincing explanations in isolation.

Conflicts continue as the world gets smaller and smaller, with the sciences, technology, and dominant societies advancing, breaching boundaries. When early tribal communes came upon confusing cultures, they pillaged and burned. This goes on even today, but with new tools and methods.

* * *

The fictional Nachiket accepted theories from books and bystanders before waking up to the conflicts and inadequacies in them. We may have mechanically imbibed some flawed views too. We may have accepted many popular theories as they help us conform.

One of the impacts of these popular theories is our accepting, without question, the purported benefits of competing and winning. This includes pressure to *succeed* at any cost and baseless fears about our condition tomorrow.

These typically prompt us to worry, compete and over-compensate on everything today for a supposedly better tomorrow. As we shall see going forward, this may be angst of no enduring usefulness.

People without proper preventive and corrective information are susceptible to psychological damage, some of which may manifest as symptoms of mental illness. We are in dire need of information that can help each of us design our individual solutions.

We need our own practical and complete worldview, unique and personal, yet compatible with others. People will have conflict and be confused if they stick to book-learning or popular thought instead of forming a broad, private, and practical worldview. A new understanding of human conflict and flawed learning can help you create this personal independent worldview and enhance *tangible* success.

Many psychosocial compulsions in our collective learning, elaborated further in the forthcoming sections, are so forceful that we need a new approach to reach the psyche enveloped in faulty understanding. This approach could be as mundane as techniques that help a person be confident or as abstract as the *meaning of life.*

ECLECTIC ESPERANTO

Section Highlights

- As we evolved, we, the human species, have absorbed some symbolism as part of our physiology or mental makeup.
- This absorbed learning is in our collective memory. It causes some people to read symbolic cues in their environment.
- The book refers to this collective memory as the collective mnemonic.
- The collective memory manifests as body language, social labeling, irrational traditional beliefs, or mystic, sometimes absurd, symbolic associations.
- When those who go primarily by theory become aware of the manifested cues, the cues can be confusing or appear to have a mystical basis.
- If we sense such manifestations, they may influence our decisions, as they suggest meaning of a different order.

Many individuals with schizophrenia see their surroundings with a heightened sense for detail. They could experience olfactory or auditory hallucinations and build delusions. Such sensing overrides the comfort one had with their personal reality before the disability's onset. The person never felt a need to question his worldview until then.

Often, afflicted individuals, caught in the novelty of the experience, construct inter-connected patterns imaginatively. They may develop delusions using these spurious connections. It is a desperate, awkwardly creative attempt to impart structure to their reality, which may appear to them as dissolving into chaos.

The inter-connectedness imparted may be as simple as reading coincidental relevance in a stranger's passing statement with one's own thoughts. Alternatively, it could be as complex as reading peculiar meaning or even hostility in physical arrangements in the vicinity.

We can extend Marshall McLuhan's insight stating schizophrenia may be a "consequence of literacy." I use this link to suggest that literacy, imprinted in us, prompts us to look for a flawed meta-meaning beyond the stated or the obvious.

Discerning this kind of underlying meta-meaning is like an individual, unable to read, guessing the story of a comic book based only on its illustrations. The conclusions reached by the individual are mostly different from the intent of the writing in it.

Individuals with schizophrenia may seek to validate this kind of meta-meaning. These individuals may have paranoid delusions that others are trying to trick them. Many people with the malady see a massive knotted-up spaghetti-like conspiracy in their situation. The person typically identifies the spouse, a neighbor, the government, a foreign power, or sometimes, a fictional being as the primary player in such conspiracies.

Granted, reams of writing on schizophrenia exist. Still, nothing comes close to explaining the strange meaning many with the condition experience. Moreover, no formal theory has admitted the existence of such unusual patterns and odd classifications, let alone attempted explanations.

Nachiket saw a strange patterning and connectivity and spiraled into a delusion that God had granted him special powers. He created the mythological Nachiketa as an alter-ego because of the out-of-the-ordinary experiences at the onset of his condition.

Can we hypothesize, taking a cue from schizophrenia, that bizarre inferences and connectivity exist and are experienced by 'normal' people too? Is there really an underlying order and meaning for us to infer? Do people show an odd symbolism today because of impressions etched on their fledgling beings?

* * *

Using current science, we are still unsure if language and symbolic patterns reside in our physiology as a species. Our genes may only facilitate our ability for language by enabling body infrastructure like the advanced human voice box. Nevertheless, consider for now a possibility that some symbolism is embedded in our physiology.

An American linguist, Noam Chomsky, has put forth similar hypotheses. Noam Chomsky proposed that Nature might pre-wire our bodies for language. He suggested that people have an innate 'language acquisition device' (LAD). This LAD could express itself as a bodily symbolism common to us all. Moreover, people could exhibit such symbolism without any external tutoring.

Chomsky gave up the LAD in favor of a 'principles and parameters' approach. He claimed there is a Universal Grammar (UG), a genetic grammar that exists in all humans.

Whether it is the LAD, UG, or something else, there seems to be some strange underlying symbolism[5]. One could propose that a patterning, a superimposed meta-meaning, is innately in our core.

Hence, there are two bases for our foundational and symbolic learning. These bases are 'individual' learning and a more extensive 'collective'

---

5   Note – the interpretations of corporal and other symbolism presented as we go ahead are the author's own extension of Chomsky's work, with no intention to undermine or distort his original analyses

learning. So, people learn symbolism and pattern recognition as individuals in their lifetime. And, we could learn as a species as well over eternity.

This distinct package of shared learning of the species could be resident in some common repository for us. To identify this repository in our discussions, we shall call it the *Collective Mnemonic* (See figure Pic. 1).

The collective mnemonic is a collection of influences that we subscribe to, often subconsciously, before we become aware. It manifests as peculiar *cues* from the surroundings.

Pic 1. The Collective Mnemonic

People sense the cues from the hypothesized collective mnemonic as unusual gestures, inordinate labeling, overlaid associations, and uncommon meanings in what is otherwise trivia.

Consider them as a perception on a plane like the unspoken *chemistry* between people. This chemistry, for example, allows people to sense fatigue or confusion by reading the body-language of others.

Some people overlay surreal meaning on the cues because they want to vindicate the new kind of sensing or awareness they have suddenly come to experience. For example, they could encounter social labels classifying individuals into predominant personality types such as *usual, real,* and *natural.*

Strange definitions label a person functioning by instincts as a *natural,* a person with a complete lack of psychic beliefs or connectedness as *real,* and persons showing typical or typified behavior as *usual.* When one senses such labeling for the first time, the person could feel diffident or taken aback.

Many sane people also find a strange double-speak in some utterances. For example, the response 'Fine!' could seem non-committal instead of affirmative. Furthermore, the mind derives meaning imaginatively using phonetic parallels. For example, 'window' could be associated with winning money or *win dough* (as tongue-in-cheek, Microsoft would readily testify!).

But these inferences are not always playful or entertaining and can sometimes be disturbing. Such deductions, often nonsensical, follow the afflicted mind's inclination to relate everything in the environment to the person's primary concerns.

Potential schizophrenia victims are generally introverts and, initially, remain unaware of the collective biases and cues around them. Some begin sensing the bias and signals for the first time, only at the onset of the psychotic condition.

In many cases, they cannot distinguish practical and valid social responses or cues from flawed or nonsensical ones. That is, aspects that can help are typically missed and bundled up with those that can harm.

* * *

Dr. Dharmaraj, our maverick psychiatrist, suggests there are subtle and obvious cues in the collective mnemonic. In support, some observed oddities lend credibility that such signals exist.

For instance, sensitive individuals may attribute subtle body language to even toddlers. A vulnerable person might conclude that toddlers unconsciously communicate using bodily postures even before learning a language! An example is when the individual ascribes meaning to toddlers patting a thigh reflexively when present during an adult conversation.

The sensitive adult interprets the toddler's action to indicate if the discussion is heading correctly. He reads the patting of the right thigh to mean 'Yes,' and the left for 'No.' The adults feel cued in despite the exchange being too complex for the toddler displaying the gesture.

We could also have seen instinctive gestures and postures in adults, playing to the state of mind or the situation. Examples are unconscious tendencies to crack one's knuckles to show agreement and rub one's palms to suggest starting afresh.

These are bodily responses to arrangements in the vicinity and lack universally deducible explanations. They reflect an obscure symbolism[6].

Some people read cues from the collective mnemonic as signs meant to communicate. Some see them as mystical prompts. Many others, as said earlier, may remain ignorant that they exist.

When sensed for the first time, such manifestations could cause feelings of confusion, inadequacy, or fear. They can block out the rational mind or, at the very least, impede its ability.

Cues from the collective mnemonic are like *Esperanto*[7] because they are known to many as a mode of communication, yet, they are still eclectic enough to prevent being systematically organized.

* * *

---

6   More examples of such connectivity because of the collective mnemonic are provided in Chapter 5, In-Sanity

7   Esperanto was an artificial language devised in 1887 conceived to bridge different European dialects

Even if Nature does not pre-wire us linguistically as a species, we could acquire specific symbolic instincts early on in our lives. History is not new for every baby born. Our reality and civilization are not new for every new birth. Therefore, we do obtain symbolic learning right from birth through social interaction.

Every age provides some tutored symbolism as instincts specific to that time. The sum of information developed until that age 'indoctrinated' the child born in the times of the Roman Empire or the Victorian era.

Our environment houses centuries of civilized thought and practices: an external storehouse. This storehouse drives early subtle conditioning in us about aspects such as competing, winning, contorted labeling, patterning, etc. It also teaches questionable practices and outdated customs of a more evident and gross nature.

Examples of that which is gross in the collective mnemonic are plentiful. They abound in religious and traditional practices. One example of a social influence from the past is the Hindu practice of isolating menstruating women.

The Hindu scriptures claim the presence of such women desecrates religious rituals. As a result, some Hindu women today take modern medicine to postpone their periods and avoid any clash with a planned religious event.

Christianity and other religions also have their share of obscure beliefs and practices. Many are left wondering if everything went right, going through rituals, and mumbling some archaic words, perhaps in Latin.

Explanations given by priests are usually inadequate and often based on unsupported symbolic associations.

The *subtle* conditioning, on the other hand, is not so widespread as the religious or gross ones. Some experience it, and some don't. It becomes palpable only under a novel kind of stress. More on this follows.

* * *

Instincts and impulses from our core are likely to be pure, as captured in some art. However, a flawed and incomplete symbolic learning, assimilated over generations, seems to have corrupted a substantial portion of the species' overall memory, or the collective mnemonic.

In its mildest form, the inability to respond to such corruption of thought causes a little anxiety or slightly irregular behavior. But, in its severe form, this could contribute to full-blown schizophrenia with delusions, hostility, and other symptoms.

Therefore, in addition to the first problem of 'flawed theory,' which presses us to compete and win, there is a close second in flawed cues from the collective mnemonic. The signals seem arranged in a bizarre and surreal order, unlike any described in books and literature.

On the positive side, such alerts may be presented by the collective mnemonic to correct deep-set personal and social trauma.

These underlying alerts or cues could be particularly frustrating for the literate when stumbled upon because they challenge the boundaries of theoretical learning. When we sense such signals for the first time, they might be shocking. For a person with schizophrenia, the cues may be hostile.

This signaling impetus, which can be flawed or valid, is experienced *differently* by everyone. This individual differentiation is another reason why the collective mnemonic defies being categorized easily. This is also why many mental afflictions are still untreatable with a medicinal magic bullet.

We will explore these ideas and provide suggestions, which should help many of us get a sense of control and poise. From this exploration and recommendations, we can close gaps between what we see and what we know about reality.

CHAPTER 2

WITHIN

Come in, Nachiket,' said the doctor and gestured for him to sit. 'I read what you have written. It is quite interesting!'

'Tell me, am I right?' Nachiket inquired, taking a seat.

'We shall see as we go on,' the doctor said disarmingly. 'How are you feeling?'

Nachiket got into the discussion straightaway. 'There is still a crowding of thoughts. You had asked me if I felt awake or asleep. The question really intrigues me as I relate it to personal awareness. How do people become aware, in their lives, well in time? Doesn't the delayed realization of my ability to be proactive put me at a disadvantage? Where is the justice, O Lord of Dharma, for I do not choose every situation I find myself?'

The doctor forced himself once more into the role, even as he wondered where this was going. 'A drive to willfully improve our situation results from us becoming aware. Until such an awakening, you had no need to question your situation or weigh your actions. You were kind of floating without a rudder. You may have been reacting diffidently and impulsively.

Now, you were reacting and not acting, Nachiket, because you accepted several social measurements. These metrics force us to pretend and conform. Such social measures and judgments are also a part of our involuntary learning. The learning happens much before we become aware of our unique capabilities to be proactive.'

Nachiket was indignant. 'The dice is loaded. Those who have been aware long before I have could downplay or impede my efforts at progress.'

'Perhaps, but consider that many of these forces result from years of social evolution,' the doctor said in a placatory tone. 'Many social devices try to provide us with a protected waiting place before we can go where each chooses. So, you must accept whatever it is currently and aim at progress. If you do not accept and aim to improve, you may stagnate or be filled with damaging thoughts.'

'So, society's declarations of what is progress, what is right and wrong, and what is desirable cause these aberrations?' questioned Nachiket.

'Not quite,' countered Dharmaraj slowly. 'As an advanced species, you did not get where you are without gathering a set of rules provided by Nature. Long before language became a given, the rules humankind lived by were akin to those of animals. This was the way the cosmos cradled you. While not apparent, such laws are also residual in you and may influence how you react.'

'Therefore, it's a double whammy! Nature and nurture force me to be abnormal before I can take control consciously,' observed Nachiket.

Dharmaraj smiled and responded. 'This is why we, the thinking and feeling human beings, seem to have developed a tool to gain and store knowledge—spoken and written language. As a human being, this tool is your birthright.'

'What about the rest of nature? Are other living beings handicapped?' asked Nachiket.

'Perhaps the venue for the human being to apply such a tool is now clear to you. Both an illiterate instinct and a literate guide are there in you. At the pinnacle of the evolutionary pyramid, the human being has a duty to himself and society and a responsibility to care for Nature.'

The doctor continued, 'There are several roles for a human being to play and several goals—personal, social, and natural. A part of popular understanding proclaims some goals as better. However, one destination is not superior to any other. How you choose to progress decides your future,' said the good doctor, putting the ball back in Nachiket's court.

'How can that be?' asked Nachiket. 'Are you saying my choices, rather than civilization's assessments, get to decide what I should do and what is success? That my choices are as valid as social norms?'

'Not entirely,' said Dharmaraj. 'I merely say the choice that you wholly own is the best. Civilization may measure success as a mix of mental, material, spiritual, or physical aims. Alternatively, it could be palpable only to you as a measure of success. Society can tailor your measure, often as a relative standard, or you can make a more enduring independent choice. You will not have internal confusion if you own your choices, social and personal, and accept the consequences.'

'...and before I learn to choose, the choices of others control me?' Nachiket concluded meditatively.

Dharmaraj smiled. 'There is a Zen saying, "When the student is ready, the teacher appears." So, until you become aware of your ability to choose, you are just not ready.'

'How can existence accommodate the choices of everybody? Are we to be eternally in conflict? Is this conflict not negative?' Nachiket queried.

'We will take this up later,' said the doctor, winding up the session. 'Answer me carefully: Do you see, hear or smell things that don't seem to have an explicit source?'

'Sometimes,' Nachiket answered. 'I hear your guiding voice and things relating to my hopes and fears, Lord.'

'Are you sleeping well?' the doctor sighed quietly and inquired.

'Yes, a little,' Nachiket said, 'but it is like an intoxicated state. I am neither awake nor asleep.'

'I am prescribing another pill you must take,' the doctor said. 'I assure you things will get clearer.'

Nachiket's parents told the doctor that Nachiket seemed calmer. He had begun eating and sleeping a little but sometimes paced furiously about the house, often at odd hours.

The doctor prescribed a very mild sedative to help Nachiket when he had difficulty falling asleep. He suggested maintaining a simple routine for Nachiket at home. The doctor also warned the parents that recovery may be slow. The family needed to be patient.

A PRIMAL PERSUASION

Section Highlights

- The collective mnemonic indoctrinates people early in their lives that they must conform to some discriminatory protocol and certain flawed social expectations.
- The belief that one needs more than others could be caused by widely prevalent comparative measures and expectations—a virtual social scorecard.
- The scorecard is insensitive and engages us in flagrant comparisons without regard for humane values.
- The scorecard and our savage illiterate natural beginnings make a humane society challenging to conceive and achieve.
- The development of literacy in our species could be part of a bigger Natural plan to disseminate environmental consciousness and ensure social harmony.

The peaks and valleys of sanity we display as a race may make us wonder: *Are we civilized?* Despite phenomenal advancements in technology and means of communication, the collective human psyche of today still has flaws. We know that the gradual development of civilization is fraught with barbarism, some of which continues into this age.

People snuffed out human life without as much thought as they would give to killing an insect, and many still do. Inhuman behavior continues to occur in this advanced age. Most of us appreciate the 'sensible' around us, although horrible news and happenings seem ubiquitous.

When we hear of atrocities such as police torture or rape, we note them and can, and should, respond with displeasure. However, if we *obsess* over them manically, it can be disturbing. It would be impossible to keep sane if negativity bombards us without limits, filtering, or safe rationalization.

Though society provides several dos and don'ts, we have been unable to successfully teach universal humane values. The continuing brutality suggests flaws in humankind's early learning, social instincts, and knowledge base.

One underlying cause of schizophrenia may be from perceiving an overwhelmingly hostile environment. Schizophrenia may arise from an inability to filter out negativity and aggression.

For instance, a person with schizophrenia might be shaken by the action of somebody aggressively drawing a chair closer. The afflicted person may not have come across or read of such an invasion of private space before and builds on it negatively to the extreme.

The patient could see it as part of a full-blown delusional conspiracy. It could cause an afflicted individual to become diffident and closed or prompt hostility. The schizophrenic condition usually precludes any rational response by the patient, such as asking the instigator the reason for the invasive action.

* * *

We are flooded with information that makes us question the adequacy of our lifestyle and contributions. Most of our sources for information compare people on ability, power, and wealth. They promote the social value placed on superiority.

Consider that even the theory of Darwinian Natural Selection is commonly misunderstood. The principle 'survival of the fittest' is sometimes skewed and applied in the social context instead of restricting it to the Natural. Norms that promote individuals or groups to be one-up on others are widely touted and unthinkingly accepted.

Much of our 'developmental' literature also focuses on our degree of *relative* success. Moreover, today's media is inclined toward highlighting such achievements. Some objects and the social status they bestow seem more desirable than others.

Many have acquired twisted and unhelpful instincts because of such misguiding information. People are normal thinkers until life suggests they have material, mental, physical, or social inadequacies compared to others. Some comparisons can make the individual reactive, downhearted or discouraged.

The corruption of our pure and gentle instincts could be a historical fact. The genesis and continuity of discontent and confusion in society seem rooted in these faulty foundations. Many simply deny their situation and respond to the environment with suspicion, aggression, and cynicism.

From this environment springs the predisposition for schizophrenia. Conversely, I suggest we can choose to learn proactively and become confident, however devastating or unstable our background or situation seems to be.

* * *

How did an aggressive philosophy promoting conflict begin? Why do some people deem it necessary? I put forth the following hypothesis: my attempt at explaining the origin of misplaced desires and, consequently, that of comparative evaluation.

This hypothesis covers the origin of our desires to become what someone else is or possess what someone else has. It attempts to explain the genesis of comparing ourselves with others. The explanation applies to the origins of desire in us as a fledgling species and its beginnings in children.

Consider that there may have been crossbreeding among early humans with discrete evolutionary paths. That is, tribes with independent origins, separated by great distances for centuries, cohabited with each other when they eventually met. This could have contributed to the availability of larger gene pools. Larger gene pools meant the potential for more advanced brain structures. Some offspring of such unions could have had the potential to be better performers.

A unique habitat could also have nurtured special survival skills in some. For example, people near water, swam, people near game, hunted, and people without shelter built rudimentary homes.

The union of independent evolutionary paths and exposure to different learning environments could have led to novel acts by a few. (Of course, in present times, in most cases, exposure and consequent insights, not the gene pool, lead to most differences in understanding and ability).

The novelty observed in a 'peer' by both the early Neanderthal of the past and the young child of today could trigger two choices. Imitate and learn the observed novel acts if inspired (or required), or ask a frustrating instinctive question—*How did he do this when I cannot?*

This forms the seed of an abstract *virtual scorecard*. Such a scorecard adds various heads, such as the extent of our understanding, possessions, wealth, power, etc., as we live. This can be the basis for many major conflicts.

The tendencies in the collective mnemonic cause such a scorecard to take shape early. Instead of having a sense of comfort, we compare ourselves with others and see relative judgments in everybody else's interactions.

This competitive scorecard may be active for many of us early in life. The scorecard may have replaced natural and helpful, albeit childlike traits such as curiosity and frankness, with impeding drives like suspicion and envy.

After flawed theory and symbolic cues, I feel the third problem for us is such a *virtual scorecard.* This scorecard prompts us to desire what someone else is or has. The scorecard, once accepted, increases in complexity as we live. It has the potential to affect all of us. The wild tendency that persists in us may not be from our savage beginnings alone. Our aggressiveness also stems from a tacit social acceptance of such a virtual scorecard.

People susceptible to schizophrenia tend to be sensitive and often feel the scorecard is unjust, whether such feelings are valid or not. This feeling was behind Nachiket's persistent one-track questioning and his attempts to blame the environment. Nachiket sensed this social pressure and scoring and felt questioning some norms will lead to answers.

* * *

Patients with schizophrenia may be delusional and extend comparative measures beyond their capacity. They could imaginatively feel part of a bigger conflict, typically beyond their ability to influence. For example, they may feel they are in the middle of a tussle between God and the devil, foreign powers and country, elitists and the commoner, etc.

Many could assume they are a part of such macrocosmic conflicts and attempt to influence them. Some become aggressive, hostile, or succumb to confusion from such delusions. Many others feel fear, envy, self-pity, and various unhelpful emotions. All this is because what one knows seems insufficient to deal with what one faces.

We can prevent or reverse such disturbances in the environment and ourselves. On the one hand, there is aggressive and savage behavior, and on the other, valuable and caring instincts, both in Nature and society's nurture.

How can we manage these two sides or persuasions of Nature and society? Are we learning intuitively as a species but with a natural and social bias to be one up distorting this learning? Do the gaps between the theoretical and practical, and the known and the unknown, need to continue? I propose some new ideas that can help us resolve such doubts. We can align individual, community, and natural directions successfully.

* * *

While Nature seems random and lawless, we can accept that its principles are survival, propagation, and balance. Lay people, as discussed earlier, tend to regard survival instinct and evolution as mechanisms to develop the toughest and the best in the species.

However, the rules of Darwinian evolution are callous about being progressive. They only ensure adaptability to the environment. Natural *law* makes do with just what is sufficient to sustain the procreation of the species. Before the advent of language, Nature was sans cultured, intellectual, or other *refined* purposes. It was and is brutal.

In an older book, *Why Things Are*, Joel Achenbach, the Washington Post columnist, said, 'Animals don't choose their behavior. Nor do they, over time, gradually learn that one strategy of behavior or growth is better. What happens is more mechanical than that. There is competition among genes.

The "good" genes, in the generic sense of good and bad, may not always win. The winner is just the one that most successfully propagates, survives, and adapts best.

Take the example of the genitalia of a drone bee exploding and injecting a virgin queen bee with sperm while effectively plugging her up from all other drones. We could agree that a gene that causes a bee to explode is bad, yet it is self-evident that the exploding-genitalia gene would win the contest because it literally shuts out the competition.

Nature is, therefore, coldly logical but extremely stupid in some sense. *Nature rewards behaviors that impede or destroy rivals (sic)*[8].'

Considering the above, *how can we care for Nature and at the same time reap its bounty? Has society nurtured a conflict with Nature? On the flip side, do our natural impulses make a humane society impossible?*

In defense of Nature, however, is its other principle: *balance.* We can look at the balance in two ways: As an inherent property of matter through 'entropy' and as housed in human beings and social systems through literacy.

Entropy is a scientific principle relating to the field of thermodynamics. This states that all physical imbalances in an isolated system balance over time. The doctor suggested that Nachiket consider another dimension of balance in Nature, like entropy, which *includes the literate human being.*

I hazard that balance in nature is inherent at one basal level—the material—through entropy. And harmony is implied at another level through the growing literacy of the human species. From one perspective, Nature is illiterate. From another, It could have facilitated the development of literacy as a harmonizing tool to enable us to look after It.

Risking being labeled *literally* elite, I venture that if wild nature suggests aggressive survival, civilized human nature offers superior balance.

Is literacy a final attempt by Nature to ensure the continuity of this ecosphere? Is literacy part of a primal persuasion, nudging us to be humane and caring? Are people responsible if this is so? Should we pause and ask ourselves: Is civilization set on a self-destruct mode?

It could be a massive problem if we continue to use our natural beginnings or material imbalances to excuse destructive and corrupt

---

8   Joel Achenbach: Why Things Are: Answers to Every Essential Question in Life; New York: Ballantine Books; 1991

behavior. Instead, we need to use this unique human literacy platform and convince ourselves to collaborate. Using literacy as a tool, we need to save the environment and our race.

In this situation, add the anxiety of unexplainable events experienced by the schizophrenia patient. He has no explanations and no solutions. Psychosocial pressures repeatedly thwart his attempts to get back on the horse. Therefore, we need the broader answers attempted in this book. Let's check out these attempts as we go on.

THE FLAWED GESTALT

Section Highlights

- The common human trauma of birthing precedes the three problems of flawed theory, illiterate symbolic cues, and society's virtual scorecard.
- These problems are the bases for inhumane, unreasonable, mystical, or superstitious behavior in otherwise 'civilized' people.
- Unless we, the afflicted and ordinary, see reasonable and collaborative living on our part as necessary, we will have damaging internal and external conflicts.

I posit that much of the deficiencies experienced, feelings of inadequacy, and lack of purpose are rooted in the problems cited. These are also the candidates contributing to the onset of schizophrenia. Despite repetitiveness, let's tie up the ideas so far.

First, we discussed that flaws in civilization's theory tend to corrupt our learning and knowledge of what we should do or achieve. Several thinkers promote winning and competing unabashedly as our only worthwhile goals.

Our thinkers may have had the right intent. Still, the existing theory is misinterpreted and fails to define and capture what really is an enduring win or accomplishment. Therefore, this has left many who should feel good about what they are, feeling short-changed instead.

Then, we talked of the possibility of an illiterate nature mimicking intelligence and passing on incorrect symbolic cues. People sense these symbolic associations under stress or in psychotic states.

We also discussed the faulty standards of success in society, which peddle virtual social scores. Many prevalent social norms of today condone damaging desires, aggressive posturing, and unreasonable behavior. These are deemed permissible if the traits conform to the social *game*.

There is more. All of us have gone through trauma in our birth experiences. The changes in our physiology while transitioning from the womb are staggering. Intra-uterine life is hugely different from life outside the womb.

The umbilical vessel spasms shut at birth, and blood no longer comes from or goes to the placenta. In addition, the following changes take place, sometimes too rapidly, causing shock:

- A hole in the heart closes.
- The lungs now inflate and oxygenate the blood.
- The liver now metabolizes.
- The kidneys filter the blood.
- The GI (gastrointestinal) tract now absorbs all nutrients.

These adaptive changes must occur systematically and place enormous demands upon the newborn. Hence, the trauma of these sudden changes could cause long-term repercussions.

We should understand that such trauma can cause incongruity in some of our early thinking and deeds. Many events happen before we realize the right thing to be or do. Some wrongdoings in our life are without any roots in our social or personal decisions but from unavoidable early trauma.

Some of the traumas occur naturally, and some are traumas from abuse. Hence, we must stop blaming ourselves exclusively. Several contributing factors in the collective mnemonic, good and bad, have made us who we are today. Therefore, we can accept, correct, or manage any wrongdoings in our past and not feel that our guilt or anger is irreparable.

* * *

Symbolic cues, introduced in the section *Eclectic Esperanto*, are the most confusing influence to understand among the four problems. This may need elaboration.

Just as human artistic expression sometimes goads our dark side, there is collective learning in us as a race, prompting us to reach disturbing conclusions. As discussed, this collective mnemonic suggests a meta-meaning in bodily gestures, strange labeling, or phonetic parallelism. It imparts a contorted significance to random stimuli and trivia in the vicinity. In addition, the mnemonic could suggest a different surreal order.

On the positive side, some of the cues from the mnemonic, one may propose, are beneficial. We need not read disturbing meanings into the *artistic language* that Nature presents through the collective mnemonic and instead see it in a positive light. For example, they may suggest ways for the experiencer to resolve early trauma or garner a new unique personal learning.

Nature does not think. Perhaps someday It will, if our ability to recall our learning as a species exceeds what we can identify as individuals. But then, why would we want it that way? Collective consciousness or intelligence that conflicts with individuality is not in order. *Why would anyone want to submit themselves to what could potentially be mindless collective conformance*[9]?

* * *

---

9   This idea of a collective drive is explored ahead in the section 'Severed Stakes

Is there an evolutionary bias in Nature nudging our species out of existence? Conversely, has Nature provided us a way to redeem ourselves through the harmonizing tool of literacy?

One side of nature conflicts with an intellectual and cultured humane outlook. Simultaneously, the natural blueprint of the species could have a redeeming feature in literacy.

The imperfect nurture of human society adds to our conflict too. Some consider notions like 'stomp out rivals and obstacles mercilessly' acceptable. They would be skeptical when confronted with the view that humanity *is required* to be humane to qualify as *normal*.

It is hard to consider that these problems exist when you are in the thick of things. We feel there is a fair degree of reason in collective thinking and its norms and that it is constantly improving. It is comforting to believe our race is rational and mature and that natural forces are gentle. But there is a valid argument for the race's core spirit or gestalt being flawed.

However, when core instincts, intellect, and interactions align, we would realize a greater altar to dedicate our existence, an altar for being humane, civilized, and socially cohesive.

Such a realization would enable us to accept ourselves, improve and perform at our best, whether afflicted or ordinary. So, let's plunge into the following sections to try and dissolve a few existential questions. We can now try and prepare firm foundations for our life's objectives.

PART II: The Preparation

In biology, all existing instincts have been grouped into two fundamental classes, according to their ends, namely, instincts for the preservation of the individual and instincts for the preservation of the species. Both cases offer aspects of the struggle, connected with transient episodes, and as it were, with encounters between the individual and the environment; and at the same time in both cases, there are instincts that show themselves as constant vital guides, with an eminently conservative function... These are the guiding instincts, with which is bound up the very existence of life in its great cosmic function... The guiding instincts, therefore, have not the impulsive character of episodic struggles, but those of an intelligence, a wisdom, leading creatures on their journey through time (the individuals) and through eternity (the species).

– Maria Montessori, (1870-1952): *The Secret of Childhood.*

CHAPTER 3

CONVERGENCE

Nachiket's parents were eager to know how long it would take him to become normal. Dr. Dharmaraj explained that psychological and physiological aspects of the problem existed. He voiced his concern that Nachiket might need intellectual mentoring as well.

The doctor asked the family to avoid discussing religion, social customs, and traditions. The trigger for the onset of Nachiket's problem seemed partly related to its unresolved issues. He needed to develop his own outlook and discover answers that made sense to him.

Nachiket was in his seat and shooting questions. 'There are times when the next steps are clear, and there are times when it is an effort just to think. A clear head is difficult to maintain. What kind of objective would help us retain our clarity?'

Dr. Dharmaraj answered with a question. 'What makes you think a perpetually clear head is a prerogative of the human species? The web of existence binds people and their minds to the physical. We cannot but feel its ramifications. Drop the thought that you must be or feel 'right' continuously. Whatever be your frame of mind, be a detached observer, and you will find the motivation to continue acting and better yourself.'

'But the condition can weigh me down...' Nachiket said.

'Not if you see a benefit,' replied Dr. Dharmaraj. 'For example, when you see yourself getting up and gaining new understanding, even in a dismal situation, you are walking the path of your chosen evolution.'

'What if my "inner witness" has deep residual impressions from the past that prevent me from walking this path?' Nachiket asked with concern.

Dharmaraj replied, 'It is one thing to say, "I cannot walk," and another to say, "I will not move." You have the programming that prevents you and the learning that enables you. Assume the forces that keep you immobile are strong. In that case, the knowledge and rewards of overcoming these forces will be extraordinary.

You can get into a state of wanting to move instead of resigning yourself to immobility. Then, your seed of willingness will sprout. You will find new ways to move, within and outside the boundaries of your residual impressions.'

'If the residual impressions are determined by tradition, culture, and other such things, these may continue to be in our environment. How can we ever overcome these?' Nachiket asked, seeming to get a hint that a fixed stance was incompatible with progress.

'They could be around you, but they would no longer hold their sway when you grant yourself the freedom of choice. A new understanding of the same things holding you back is inevitable once you permit yourself to grow. After all, what are tradition, culture, and other forces of civilization but the human species in motion over time? You have made them fulfill their purpose as the cradle of your understanding when you appreciate these forces as things you must build upon.' Dharmaraj pushed to drive home the point he wanted to make.

Nachiket nodded and said, 'In effect, I could have a problem that is also a foundation...'

'Right! Hindu philosophy gave you the notion that people are reborn, but we must play our current role to advance. This role is not a compromise but a validation of what we ought to be. So, if I asked you to consider that you are the Nachiket of this present time and not someone reborn, how would it make you feel?' The doctor put this question casually but was tense, gripping the arms of his chair. There could be hostility at his suggestion, but the doctor guessed the ground was prepared for a positive response.

Nachiket responded quite calmly, 'A little different. What will happen if my current and earlier lives conflict?'

'They need not be.' Dharmaraj said, relieved that Nachiket's response was not hostile. This meant that Nachiket could yet pull out of his delusion. 'You are a repository of concepts. Once you realize that certain concepts and ideas can be valid for anyone, it is easier to accept them regardless of their source.'

Nachiket continued, remaining unaffected. 'Lord, if the concepts are supreme, all of us should be convinced. None of us should be disagreeing with another...'

Dharmaraj realized he would have to bide his time for now. He continued explaining, 'The concept is the same, but how we actualize it could be different. A set of abilities and inclinations particular to an individual determine the actualization. It is as if we are all walking different paths to get to our special destinations. What is common is that we are all moving a step closer.'

Nachiket asked, 'What determines our path and inclinations?'

Dharmaraj introduced the concept of inner intent. 'We have within us innate learning. It is as if there is a spore in us waiting for the right conditions. When our chosen purpose aligns with our experience, it leads to easy success. When we lack this kind of purpose, it can lead to conflict. Our alignment with a clear inner intent will release our true abilities.'

'How do I recognize this in myself?' Nachiket asked anxiously.

The doctor pressed home the headway being made, 'When you have completely come to the present and feel each day builds on the previous one, you will feel secure in your intent.'

Nachiket then asked, 'What do I do in the meantime? How do I know I am headed in the right direction?'

Dharmaraj had only one answer. 'Use humanity as a sounding board for your intentions until you recognize the personal benefit in any outcome. This means that faith in the grace of time needs to be a conscious decision.

See any conflict as guiding towards consistently improving—the way to an inherent, congruous state, even if it is presently impalpable. See the conflict and confusion as temporary teachers. Act for now with the volition feasible.'

'Then what about spontaneity in action? If I pause to weigh everything, I will not be spontaneous,' Nachiket said, thinking of the times he had acted, secure in his spontaneity.

'The difference is that you can trust your actions as constructive when spontaneity comes from healthy instincts,' the doctor explained.

'What about when others try to force their ideas on me or influence my instincts?' Nachiket worriedly asked.

'Ideas around you are just inputs,' Dr. Dharmaraj reassured Nachiket. 'You must decide what you accept or would like to stand for. We will talk about this sometime.'

Dr. Dharmaraj could see the medicine was working, but his interactions with Nachiket were intense. The doctor found he had to think rapidly to answer Nachiket's probing questions. The discussions clearly indicated a person within, trying to make sense of a confusing plethora of theories and perceptions.

The doctor had suggested that Nachiket's delusion was invalid, knowing anything beyond a suggestion could trigger hostility. Dr. Dharmaraj wondered how much longer he would have to keep up his charade of divinity and how Nachiket would feel when he ended it.

THE YELLOW BRICK ROAD

Section Highlights

- We can align conflicting instincts and reason by having a broader personal intent.
- The intensity of intent ensures our acts are sustainable, result-oriented, and excellent.
- When personal purpose and intent include larger goals, we experience an extraordinary synergy and a significant ability for success.
- Recognizing such a personal purpose and intent early on in life rarely happens because people perceive conflicting forces.

Consider that children are bundles of instinct and reason. If a child's nurture fails to teach responsible behavior, the child will explore the world of 'bad' instincts. For example, when a ball bounces onto the middle of the road while playing, the child can learn to ask for an adult's help despite a pressing need for the toy.

The best role instinct can perform for an adult is that of a 'sensing' mechanism. We pass on the sense to our reason to process. If logic validates the instinct, we can act on it. If it does not, we *should* reject it. This then becomes an intelligent, proactive choice.

Whether ordinary or afflicted, such a choice could seem like a tall order for us. Nevertheless, we can acquire the skill and wisdom to help us decide when to hitch a ride on our instincts and when to get off. One can understand when to be detached from instincts and when to go with their flow.

A person cannot let any flawed conditioning in his past affect how he spontaneously and instinctively reacts today. Instead, it is better to learn from the past to help weigh decisions rationally and act. Then, choice backed by experience can become a path for spontaneity with greater relevance to the present.

We may feel the making of thought-out choices conflicts with spontaneity. However, an informed choice is more relevant and covers a larger context than impulsive and intuitive action[10]. Therefore, while recognizing its value, we cannot assume spontaneity is always helpful.

A person may make incorrect decisions because instincts are often flawed, especially for an afflicted person. But on the other hand, if we have very well-honed and proven instincts, we can arrive at a reasonable decision to trust them. A simple test is to recollect how often you have acted on hunches and been comfortable with the consequences.

* * *

Our instincts emerge from deeper impressions. These are the 'residual impressions' etched in us, referred to by Dr. Dharmaraj. Some of these imprints trigger instincts that act against personal betterment. They may force the afflicted to stay constrained within the symptoms of schizophrenia.

No matter how (in) appropriate your instincts are, they are the primary influencers of action in abrupt situations. Therefore, nursing back to health instincts that are in error becomes vital. We usually regret impulsive actions, but they do not create regrets if instincts are aligned with a larger purpose.

We can realign our stray impulses by acquiring a new perspective. A robust set of instincts would help focus actions with their subtle presence. When we nurse these *tendencies* of the mind to be healthy, they aid us in making the right choices.

How do we train and align instincts? We *must first be willing* to move in a progressive direction (the means) despite personal betterment (the ends) being invisible now.

---

10 The terms 'context' or 'contextual' are used in the book to indicate a focus on the real, rational and constructive. Our focus is not mystical, parochial or harmful.

This direction is much like the Yellow Brick Road to the Emerald City in the children's classic, *The Wizard of Oz*. The principal characters set out on this road to find some things, which they eventually discover, they already have.

Dorothy realizes she already has a way to get back to Kansas. The Tin Man discovers he is not heartless. The cowardly lion finds out he is courageous. The straw-filled scarecrow learns he is brainy anyway. Besides, the wizard, who turns out not to be a wizard, only provides a symbolic token of a reward for their quest.

This willingness to believe in something and plow ahead is how we can *reverse engineer* and nullify flawed instincts. Our willingness and intent are potent drivers for promoting good instincts and success. They feed the focus and effort that get results.

A half-hearted intent only produces half-hearted acts that fail. The greater the willingness and intention are, the greater the effort. Consequently, the quality of decisions, actions, and results is also better. *The strength of intent will enable us to move our muscles and get results.*

This is what Dr. Dharmaraj was referring to as *wanting* to move. Even if the initial situation is shabby, there is a tendency towards excellence or betterment when there is an appropriate intent. You can always get it right at some point if you keep in mind the right driving goal.

With solid intent, you follow through with appropriate action. We cannot ignite such a powerful intent when our expectations are narrow. However, we would develop this vital drive when we get concerned and feel responsible for a broader range of things. Such a comprehensive intent would even hone our instincts to function like on autopilot in many matters.

Everyone participates in our purpose when we are inclusive. Others buy-in because they are also a part of the goal. There is a great synergy to tap into when you commit that a broad range of issues will improve, not just your personal ones.

* * *

We may disagree with others on whether things must get better, how much better they must get, and sometimes *how* they must get better. Still, such conflicts would be resolved when the purpose includes a concern for issues beyond the immediate self.

Finding a personal purpose and intent early on in life rarely happens because people see dividing walls and conflicting directions all around. However, we can resolve perceived dichotomies, such as spirituality and pleasure, selfishness and altruism, nature and the intellect, haves and have-nots, etc.

Such divides get resolved if, instead of seeing conflict, we remain constructive and starve the destructive forces. Then, any broad enough and inclusive personal purpose would align, I would say inevitably, to human, humane and productive goals.

In fact, all that may be required for us to discover our personal purpose is a catalyst in the form of self-awareness. We all have it, while it may be dormant in a few. When you focus on the context and stay with the big picture, the trivial things on your way will be irrelevant.

Many of the afflicted are stuck questioning trivialities when they should align with higher contextual goals. The following section discusses a set of generalized divisive forces that influence us. These divisions make it difficult for us to walk the yellow brick road.

SEVERED STAKES

Section Highlights

- We will find motivation when we subscribe to a more inclusive set of concerns.
- Analyzing individual, natural, and collective drives reveal that being constructive along all three is truly humane.

- Being destructive along any of the three drivers is the antithesis of humane intent and invariably precipitates conflict.
- To experience holistic personal motivation, we must subscribe to a broad driving intent.

Only a few shining exceptions among us define their purpose early in life. So, what happens to the rest of us who are muddling through? Religion and theology provide some tentative rules and abstract explanations for the purpose of life. This keeps several people content and gives them the patience to wait for concrete 'proof.'

Even so, conflicting ideas in religion or ideology are often the trigger for a schizophrenic episode. Harsh as this seems, we should understand that finding logical solutions in faith is impossible. At best, I suggest that the hopeful amongst us can do better by postponing the attempt until a sense of readiness.

Religious beliefs can collapse under close logical questioning if one is not primed with faith. When we are ready, religion happens—or *unhappens*. Nonetheless, it is best to keep faith when you already have faith. It always helps. Religion and belief provide foundational support that aids the gradual development of personal ideologies, sometimes beyond religious boundaries.

We will explore tradition later as a complete chapter. Meanwhile, here is a peek at an ideological range without theological overtones. This should help in recognizing a broader personal purpose.

Dr. Dharmaraj explained to Nachiket that the power of ideas is autonomous. It was part of the effort to woo him from his delusional persona. Accordingly, the following analysis is also autonomous, objective, and independent, presented with the intent to highlight divisive personal drivers within us.

* * *

Multi-dimensional drivers influence our minds. Three of the apparent dimensions are those of our individuality, community, and nature. I have tried to analyze these using a quasi-technical framework. I try capturing several ideologies along three axes of *individuality*, *community*, and *nature* as a 3-dimensional model.

The illustration (Table 1): *The Axes of Ideology*, identifies these 3-D axes with the letters 'I' for the Individual, 'C' for Community, and 'N' for Nature. When a plus sign (+) is placed after the letter, it indicates a constructive outlook along the axis. When a minus sign (−) is placed after the letter, it shows a destructive or apathetic tendency along the axis. To illustrate, 'C+' means constructive, and 'C−' means destructive or apathetic along the community axis.

The three axes of individual, community, and nature, along with their two constructive and destructive orientations, would result in eight positions in the 3-dimensional model. Combinations of I, C, and N, with plus (constructive/ positive) and minus (destructive/ apathetic), result in eight dominant states. Let us explore what the states represent.

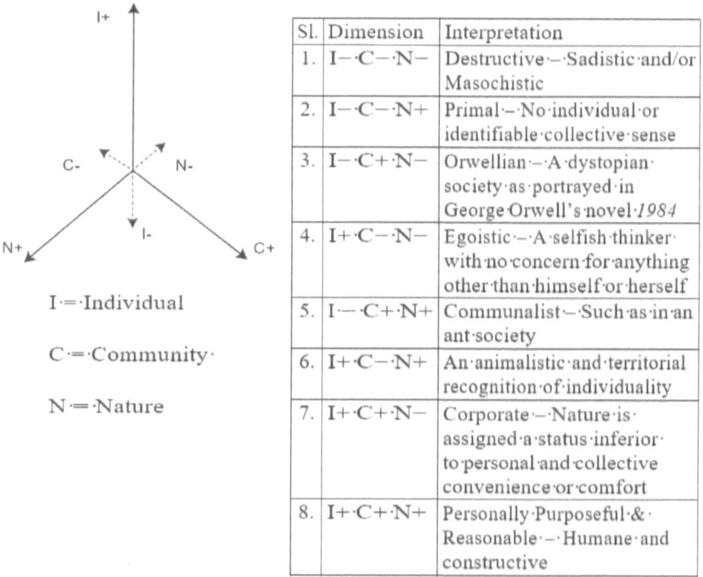

Sl.	Dimension	Interpretation
1.	I− C− N−	Destructive — Sadistic and/or Masochistic
2.	I− C− N+	Primal — No individual or identifiable collective sense
3.	I− C+ N−	Orwellian — A dystopian society as portrayed in George Orwell's novel *1984*
4.	I+ C− N−	Egoistic — A selfish thinker with no concern for anything other than himself or herself
5.	I− C+ N+	Communalist — Such as in an ant society
6.	I+ C− N+	An animalistic and territorial recognition of individuality
7.	I+ C+ N−	Corporate — Nature is assigned a status inferior to personal and collective convenience or comfort
8.	I+ C+ N+	Personally Purposeful & Reasonable — Humane and constructive

Table 1. The Axes of Ideology

We begin with the totally negative state, negative along all 3 axes. The 'I– C– N–' is an entirely destructive state, perhaps pure evil. The second state, 'I– C– N+', indicates the condition of a primal entity having no individual or collective goals. It applies to a life force fueled by elementary nature; an example is unicellular lifeforms. They do not show any distinct individual traits.

The Orwellian state (I– C+ N–) is based on the author George Orwell's portrayal of a fictional society. In this, a dictator quashes individual freedoms and natural urges for what is deemed to be a collective benefit.

For the egotist (I+ C– N–), there is a concern for just the self and no other sense of responsibility. Such a person is insensitive when it comes to community or nature.

The next position is that of an entity showing no individual traits but is communalist (denoted by I– C+ N+). This mode has a group or collective objective but no individual distinction. For such entities, existence is like an ant colony, never questioning natural and collective urges such as foraging for the colony. Such entities may have no sense of individuality but have enough collective acumen to survive as a species.

An animalistic outlook (I+ C– N+) refers to an instinct for survival as a solitary entity with boundaries marked naturally. This bestial entity cannot subscribe to a higher 'civic,' communal, or intellectual direction.

Next, in the 'Corporate' state (I+ C+ N–), a tendency to promote convenience sacrifices Nature. This state primarily panders to whatever aids the immediate comfort of the individual and the community. This is often at loggerheads with Nature. It tends to be ecologically destructive. Several of humanity's pursuits are hedonistic and with no care for the future of our world if we are comfortable today.

As we confront life, most personal actions or thoughts lean towards one of these combinations. Specifically, instincts for self-preservation, I and N, put up walls against C's positive influence. Some people see their obligations as part of a civilized race to be compromising self-preservation. Many see a broad acceptance of different social sub-groups as a threat.

Due to varying degrees of personal alignment with the I, C, and N directions, several social and political factors divide instead of uniting us. Society seems splintered in its ideologies. As a result, we cannot conceive and achieve a planet-wide responsible human civilization. The stakes we have, as human beings, seem severed.

Dr. Dharmaraj explained to Nachiket that a broader civilized personal purpose includes self-preservation. He implied that a negative orientation on even one of the discussed dimensions has damaging repercussions.

Acceptance of communal diversity enables harmonious individual living with a civil attitude of mutual respect and unity. Nobody in this age of interdependence can afford to negatively affect the global community and Nature.

A purposeful direction betters all three facets of individual, community, and nature (I+ C+ N+). Such an inclusive purpose, I believe, will ensure our sustenance and survival, both as individuals and as a species.

* * *

How do we choose and invest our efforts when we see several options with several valid arguments? I see disagreement as also having a purposeful role. We shall see how personal purpose exists despite conflict, and we will know the importance of debate itself.

LEGACY AND LEARNING

Section Highlights

- Many imbibe flawed social learning and protocol because they are not aware early enough in their lives.
- We cross over to awareness by acknowledging that some part of us is inevitably getting better, following an innate personal purpose.

- A new perspective can rid us of the tricky part of our legacy and help develop an awareness of our personal purpose.
- We align with such an innate personal purpose with growing awareness and knowledge.

As expressed before, many amongst us have just trusted the environment despite its flaws. This may have led to harmful experiences sometimes. A school of Primal Therapy claims that injuries to personal cognitive integrity could result from internalizing a flawed and unrealistic schema[11].

Similarly, I speculate that a mind cannot be a clean slate even at birth. The conditioning in our past, beginning with the womb itself, may be contorted and burdensome for some of us. Many only build on a flawed history and never break free. Having an open mind would hence be difficult until our past is resolved.

A legacy influenced Nachiket, his thoughts, words, and deeds before he could develop the ability to weigh the pros and cons. It is so for every one of us. Our legacy needs tempering by learning.

* * *

Dr. Dharmaraj pointed out that Nachiket would carry a load of his past until he realized it involved many things outside his control. We may never be able to address the last of the four problems, our birth trauma.

Despite efforts by science to make birthing as free of trauma as feasible, it cannot prevent the shock. This trauma explains some of the innate *abnormalities* we inevitably need to manage.

---

11 Paraphrasing from Stettbacher, Konrad: Making Sense of Suffering: The Healing Confrontation with Your Own Past. New York, N.Y., U.S.A. Meridian, 1993

However, not all is dismal. Cognitive learning that is contextual directs us towards our personal purpose.

We can let go of everything unhelpful in our past if we realize that we did not and cannot always choose with complete awareness. Nonetheless, we have some specific and unique seed awareness that guides us towards betterment.

In other words, our intrinsic core is inexorably getting better by some measure.

Call it wisdom, call it awareness, call it evolution, or call it the path of the soul. There should be no confusion regarding this primary direction. *Things get better innately in some manner.* When we are ready, we can experience it.

Despite an inadequate present, positive change is inevitable with a broad canvas for betterment. We learn to celebrate growth with some belief and commitment. We can don an outlook that everything will improve. We can get our answers.

Anyone can discover personal purpose by acknowledging growth. As we go on, Nachiket finally sees that he is where he is because of all that he had to go through. I continue to live *and seek* my purpose, deficiencies, and all, just like the fictional Nachiket.

Picture and revel in the idea that someone, somewhere, sometime is proud of you. Even before becoming aware of it, you can celebrate a belief that you are getting better, that you are getting proactive, and that you are at peace. Expect this.

But, first, let's see the fundamental principles that make it possible for us to be proactive, understand our uniqueness, and know betterment. Then, we can see how to acknowledge our specific and constantly progressive personal purpose.

* * *

In the next part of the book, in addition to providing more hints on acknowledging personal purpose, we will explore our three addressable problems. These 'disorienters' are flawed theory, symbolism, and the scorecard (the fourth problem of birthing and infantile trauma can be managed to a certain extent by resolving the *other* three). We will see how to deal with the direct repercussions of these 'disorienters' in Part III of the book.

PART III: The Solution

The demand to be free is the cause of your problems. You want to see yourself as free. The one that is saying 'You are not free' is the same one that is telling you that there is a state of 'freedom' to be pursued. But the pursuit is slavery, the very denial of freedom. I do not know anything about freedom, because I do not know anything about myself, free, enslaved, or otherwise. Freedom and self-knowledge are linked. Since I do not know myself and have no way of seeing myself, except by the knowledge given to me by my culture, the question of wanting to be free does not arise at all. The [preconceived] knowledge you have about freedom denies the very possibility of freedom. When you stop looking at yourself with the knowledge you have, the demand to be free from that self drops away.

– U.G. Krishnamurthy (1916–2007) in *Mind is a Myth*

CHAPTER 4

EXTERIOR

Dr. Dharmaraj knew that Nachiket's recovery required overcoming the positive symptoms (like hallucinations) with medication and resolving the negative symptoms (like social withdrawal) with fresh thinking[12].

Recovery usually needs patients to gain enough insight to look at their symptoms with adequate detachment. But first, the doctor was keen to tackle the positive symptoms as they were the bigger impediment.

'How are you, Nachiket? Are the voices continuing?' Dharmaraj smiled and asked, gesturing to a chair.

'Yes. Faintly...like murmurs,' Nachiket replied, settling in. 'However, I clearly hear a boy's voice from back in high school. I used to constantly compare myself with him.'

'What does *it* say?' the doctor continued.

'I think he says I am a loser and will never amount to anything in life... It's not very clear...' fumbled Nachiket.

'And what do you feel about this?' said Dharmaraj, in typical psychiatric fashion.

'I feel our discussion will solve this. Winning seems to be everything in life...,' Nachiket stated, letting the words dangle.

---

12 For other examples of Positive and Negative symptoms of schizophrenia, please visit the Preface

Dharmaraj once again picked up the threads, 'Okay, here goes... If winning is everything, then everything must win. This is not just a play of words but reflects the "win-win" attitude at the heart of success. Your earlier questions on conflicts of choice have a potential answer in this overarching question: Do your choices and their outcome depend purely on *another*?'

'But isn't this true about winning?' Nachiket countered, catching on fast. 'There can only be one clear winner in any game or sport.'

Dharmaraj smiled again and replied, 'A man said, "If your happiness depends on what somebody else does, I guess you do have a problem.[13]" When your focus is not on winning, but on another losing... that is a problem.'

'But how can one win without another losing?' quizzed Nachiket.

'In the game of existence—if you can even call it a game—there are no losers. Humankind has glorified its winners as examples, not because the others should give up and turn away. The problem multiplies because many of us think those who do not win are losers; they just fade into nothing.

Instead, the truth is many can live equally satisfying lives by choosing to participate in their own independent dimension of success. The secret to winning is the continuity of our confident drive as a player.'

'Do you say that winning for a cause is also pointless? Why put in any effort at all then?' asked Nachiket.

'Now you see the importance of a bigger altar,' Dharmaraj responded. 'It is the stubborn insistence of playing within narrow, defined boundaries that may be our undoing. You win or lose for a cause only because you accept what others have defined as a victory, preventing you from acquiring a *sense* of winning.'

---

13 Bach, Richard: Illusions, The Adventures of a Reluctant Messiah. New York: Delta, 1998

'But is it not decided in some way? I do not choose to lose—it happens,' said Nachiket.

'If you think you have lost... you have well and truly lost,' said Dr. Dharmaraj gently but firmly. 'You can act on the circumstances in which you find yourself. You can open new opportunities. It is impossible to lose, except by your choice to remain in an unpleasant situation that you find yourself.'

'Lord, if you choose to foist a situation upon me, what can a mere mortal do?' Nachiket said submissively, still addressing the doctor as divine.

Dharmaraj sighed unobtrusively at being addressed in this fashion but continued, 'To see the gain in any situation, we need to turn obstacles into stepping-stones. One must take ownership first and come out of fear and self-doubt. When people are willing to change their circumstances, things that seem magical happen.

When we are willing, we notice things around us that will help us. We observe opportunities clearly and are awake to the chances of turning a situation around with the force of our willingness. A mortal is not mere, but a bundle of progressive choices waiting to happen.'

'But sometimes the way people want things to happen and how they actually turn out are different...' said Nachiket, stating a common frustration.

'We don't live in a perfect world. Based on experience, others read our actions and reach independent conclusions. However, if you have provided enough valid options and communicated effectively, the results of your actions will be within expectations.

You must see it only as requiring yet another action when they are not. You cannot control all your environment's responses, but you have some control over what you can influence.'

The doctor answered using a version of the Hindu concept of the difference between fate and the outcome of personal action.

'How do I know the difference between what can be influenced and what cannot?' Nachiket asked, still seeming to refuse ownership of his freedom to choose.

'When you create enough options for others to choose from, you can influence their decisions,' the doctor said emphatically. 'This requires action and effort.'

'And if the rules for me and around me change?' Nachiket questioned, realizing where the conversation was headed and almost talking to himself.

'You have just answered the question with that question,' the doctor said, smiling. 'That then is a situation where you must seek and adopt new definitions of success, a situation where you change too.'

'Can I choose my future, considering what has happened to me in my past life?' asked Nachiket, convinced on the issue.

'Yes!' Dharmaraj exclaimed. 'You can choose a future, exclusively yours, if you do not compare or confuse it with anyone else's life. For the unique you, it would get better, in some manner or another... *if* you choose to make it so and appreciate any outcome.'

'But I am afraid. Is there no foundation to my thinking?' Nachiket sounded worried. 'I feel like I am falling without a safety net. What is happening to me? How long will it take me to adapt?'

'Let's explore this a little more. In our next meeting, perhaps... Yes?' the doctor posed gently. 'You will see it is not so much "Why?" or "What?" but that the point is to go forward. You are not alone in feeling fear when facing what seems new. You cannot banish fear but need to manage it instead. I will teach you some things to do when you are afraid. You will learn and adapt. Perhaps slowly... but definitely.'

To understand that there was nothing to fear, Nachiket had to learn some coping strategies. He needed techniques that would help him overcome his timidity and the fear of being in what was a novel environment[14].

Dharmaraj told Nachiket's parents that returning to an everyday social life might take longer. Nachiket would first need to develop a new outlook to help him be confident.

JONESES SYNDROME

Section Highlights

- The first complication in the jumbled bag of theory is its ideas about winning and competition.
- Time has twisted Darwin and Adam Smith's macro-theories of 'survival of the fittest' and 'competitive markets' to apply them in the micro to individuals.
- The social environment of this age does not always support merit and justice. It lacks a level playing field, unlike sports.
- Social elitism encourages relative stature and sidelines challenges to the status quo.
- We eliminate unnecessary mental baggage when we anchor in absolute personal betterment instead of relative victories.
- We achieve this by realizing the uselessness of tying our self-esteem to others.

The following thoughts would be labeled 'leftist' by society's grouping or the social taxonomy. Social taxonomy prompts us to label and file, within its available definitions, anything outside of the existing order. This is a way society maintains the status quo.

Nachiket, like several of the afflicted, perceived this social labeling and pointed it out as an injustice. This is because he had no lexicon to help

---

14 See RI 1 "Flying Above the Flak" at the end of the book under Recovery
    Instruments

him understand the labeling. But we can transcend much labeling and stereotypes to get a sense of identity. Adopting a new outlook would enable us to be in the 'madding crowd' yet stand apart from its madness.

Recall that you got a new take on problems in the book's first two parts and considered a few unusual thoughts. This sharing was to highlight flaws in nature and nurture. Many personal doubts and collective constraints carried over from the past manifest today in our thoughts, words, and deeds.

This Part addresses three problems contributing to negative feelings: flawed theories, illiterate symbolic cues, and civilization's virtual scorecard. The negatives have the potential to trigger mental afflictions such as schizophrenia.

* * *

Theory and history housed in the postulated collective mnemonic are tricky. Some of history's forces are appropriate, while some are not. Proper influences guard humane aspects like dignity, individual freedom, and self-esteem. But several norms carried forward into this age by us as a society clash with these aspects.

Earlier in the book, I suggested that the collective mnemonic is a source of symbolic cues. In addition, this source also preserves *constricted* definitions of success. An embedded repository promotes the winning of some at the cost of others. The repository glosses over the loss of others as collateral damage. This aggressive age has twisted the meaning of victory to make a virtue of a misguided truth.

The focus of this chapter is hence on what I see as flawed conclusions regarding competition and winning. The chapter highlights society's role in conditioning us to accept that some end results are superior. Among those that have contributed to these suspect conclusions are our success gurus.

Some gurus have done extensive and indiscriminate selling of competing and winning. Social conditioning and widespread belief point to the quantum of wealth, fame, or luxury as the valid yardsticks of success. Straightaway, such measures deny a sense of satisfaction to several contributions essential to the working of society.

All of us have experienced the more superficial manifestations of such core conditioning. For instance, we seek lists of the 'Top Ten Blondes,' or the wealthiest, beyond entertaining interest. We compare. The need for comparisons is ubiquitous and reflects a widespread craving for superlative icons.

Our social tutoring and rewarding mechanisms compel people to compete for relative superiority. The conditioning and cues are so pervasive that they would hinder anybody's constructive efforts toward holistic personal wellness.

Entire societies, such as the American and Swiss, have ostensibly developed around the principle: *To each his own.* Not a bad idea if it catches on in the true sense. Most forget this and focus excessively on winning THE prize because it seems the winner takes all.

Such beliefs create the fanatic, be it a foaming-at-the-mouth greedy business executive, a bigoted sociopath, a jihadi terrorist, or anyone who desires absolute victory over others. Such people accept definitions of success popularized by the wizards of propaganda. This propaganda asks them to destroy rivals and spreads a divisive splintering of society.

* * *

Prevalent norms would have us believe that those who possess the most social trophies are winners in life. This means society constantly reinforces the idea that 'ordinary' people are undeserving and cannot feel a sense of fulfillment. There is constant pressure to play catch up. Instead, what if we realize that everyone is average or 'lacking' at something?

At the risk of sounding iconoclastic—even movie stars, Olympic athletes, and Presidents of nations are average. All of us are human and fallible and average in many aspects. We should attach no stigma to *averageness*. It is not about professing, 'I am humble,' then being maleficent like Dickens' character Uriah Heep in the classic *David Copperfield*. It is about feeling blessed, equitable, and a part of humanity.

Being 'average' in some respects and whole-heartedly accepting this about others and ourselves helps us live life to the fullest; without feeling that something is lacking. It has nothing to do with our possessions, performance, or pride.

Pause and look at yourself in a mirror. Can you look at yourself without criticism and yet be modest? Can you believe you are average and still feel blessed and unique? When recognized volitionally and applied without bias, such an insight would bolster resilient self-esteem.

* * *

Civilization will seem inherently unfair if we base our sense of justice on the popular instead of the personal. The 'winners' want the rest to believe that life is a game where the best things are only for the best players. This is the only way they can label their position as winners or as the 'best,' regardless of whether the value they have to offer is commensurate or questionable.

We will feel inadequate if we base our success and state of mind on the popularly touted benefits of competing alone. Consider that a premium car, an elaborate house, or expensive holidays are among the ways you feel others are at an advantage. This, then, is a way that makes you think you are a loser...and you are a loser—when you stick to these terms.

The collective mnemonic's fallacy of defining success on the wrong ideals has left a majority feeling inadequate and yearning for more. It also remains impossible for the 'top percentage' to be permanently content. This is because the accepted definitions of success constantly shift, or replace, the standards we subscribe to concerning what we should be, do or have.

Initially, Nachiket had it figured out and felt his ability, adequate effort, and the 'known' ways of justice would produce favorable results. There was no need to doubt the volumes of fiction and non-fiction literature that had declared 'proven' ways to succeed.

Perhaps armed with academic learning, we feel reason and order rule supreme. However, when a person who is only academically tutored becomes aware, he might see the environment as extremely critical and unfairly competitive. I confess that it was far beyond anything I had imagined from within the safety of my home and academia.

Most people, on becoming aware, quickly toe the line of popular protocol or accept what is often a laidback lifestyle and profession (according to accepted social standards). However, they may still think what they are is inadequate.

Competition exists, fair and foul. We cannot dismiss destructive conflict and rabid competition. These must be accepted. But a personal competitive philosophy will create proactive terms for us to go with the uncommon and yet, tolerate the common in the ways of winning and losing.

There is an alternative proactive attitude we can develop instead. This attitude would help us realize and accept, without any doubt, that we get what we deserve. We can feel deserving without feeling pressured by what others have, now or ever. This philosophy, I believe, can support us in recognizing our own niche success.

* * *

Two scientific stalwarts, Charles Darwin and Adam Smith, have suggested that competitiveness and comparison are inherent in society and essential survival mechanisms. Popular thought claims 'The best succeed' as the message of these stalwarts. Hence, our age emphasizes competition and winning to such a degree that it is easily misunderstood.

We have already discussed the stupidity of taking Darwin's theory of evolution in flora and fauna and applying them to the literate and civilized human race (the example of the drone bee[15]). Further, Adam Smith's perfect markets, in which competition and meritocracy are almost synonymous, do not hold water.

Many of our markets suppress entities that can add commendable value to society. As a result, several genuine social groups may be passed over because they lack the 'cash' or the 'right connections' to sustain or continue.

Adam Smith believed that resources are scarce, and Darwin said only the environmentally fittest survive. 'Scramble and fight for the crumbs,' they seemed to say. People have forgotten that there is enough for all on the table. Externalities like the media, the market, and (tongue-in-cheek) the mother-in-law control our wants instead!

* * *

One-upmanship is a trait, a historical urge, seeded in several people. One-upmanship is an outward expression of a strong need to establish relative superiority.

Present-day advertising exemplifies—and perhaps legitimizes—this one-upmanship. Most advertising tries to create a sense of inadequacy or 'need' in the buyer by comparing products and people to one another to force a buying decision. Some advertisers also put down competing products instead of just promoting the pluses of whatever they are pitching.

To be superior, as the word implies, requires *relative* measures. However, we are not talking about goods and services here, but about

---

15 As explained earlier, the genitalia of a mating drone bee explode and inject the virgin queen bee with sperm, also effectively plugging her up from all other male drones' sperm

thinking and feeling beings. Therefore, a survival strategy based purely on conquest *destroys* others in the wake of competing.

Competing in the common vein also advocates the kind of 'killer instinct' popularized by sport. This promotes the instinct to defeat or have no mercy. Take, for example, the practice of 'sledging' in the game of cricket. This practice uses taunts to unsettle the opponents' minds. As a result, children who play the game sometimes see sledging as acceptable but cheating as not.

Some people carry the 'killer instinct' outside the sports arena. For people who are innocent theorists or are blind to life as it really is, experiencing this 'killer instinct' can be a shock and a challenge. They wake up to the fact that it can be a wild world where 'it's hard to get by just upon a smile.'[16]

Popular thought encourages one-upmanship and the killer instinct in this aggressive age. Unfortunately, individuals soaked in these traits use effort to find original ways to unnerve their opponents. They are blind to the benefit of developing their own skills or any value-addition they can bring. When we compete to win instead of competing to deliver excellence, one-upmanship and the killer instinct become tools.

Competition helps deliver excellence. However, this idea of merit may take a back seat when winning is the only incentive. There is pressure created by the focus on winning alone, by the idea that second place is for the first loser. Nature tells us to block rivals in evolution. Additionally, collective understanding tells us to compete aggressively to succeed.

Strong urges to compete and to win decisively therefore exist. Both the illiterate natural force and a collective confusion about the idea of competition promote such desires. This causes people to consider foul

---

16 From the song "Wild World" by the British singer-songwriter Cat Stevens aka Yusuf

means on par with the fair. Unlike sport, which provides a level playing field, society maximizes differences in opportunity.

* * *

A few celebrities are showcased with a boy/girl-next-door aura, implying that anybody from the masses can make it. The 'powers that be' gently push an elitist agenda, a separation that promises select benefits solely for being one-up. Such a discriminatory game of life provides distracting crumbs and promises based on relative stature while subtly imposing one-upmanship.

Sports *can* be compared to life for a different reason—the antithesis of their purported end. Sports are good because they teach us sportsmanship. They teach us that losing can be fair and is not the end of the world.

Sporting champions lose, sometimes more often than they win. But nevertheless, they still inspire us to newer successes and better things without losing heart. This is the only learning from sport to be applied to life. In our average or ordinary lives, there would be nobody to knock into a bloody pulp. There are no championships to win or trophies to flaunt in life, as in games and sports. There is no enduring end *game*.

The characteristic reaction to such a statement will usually be disagreement. This is because years of conditioning by sensationalist media have caused us to liken life to sports. They promote the obsession with being ahead, which can be an unnecessary and troublesome mindset in the long haul. It is an addiction that is hard to kick. Many forsake common civilities for the prize because of the conditioning that life is a frivolous game anyway.

Most of us see sports positively and remain aware that they are for fitness, camaraderie, and entertainment. The idea is we play 'No games, just sports!'[17] We don't indulge in destructive acts or play unnerving 'games'

---

17 A fictitious tagline for a sports shoe from the movie What Women Want (2000)

to stay ahead. While we can keep the progressive aspects of the analogy between sports and life, we must avoid treating life as 'Just a game!'[18]

Organizations, too, may be ruthless in their pursuit of success. They may lack a higher and more humane purpose. The 1975 Norman Jewison film, *Rollerball*, depicted this. In this film, monopolistic corporations of the future promote a ruthless and bloody full-contact game—yes, a game—called Rollerball. It is the prime distraction for the masses. There are no governments, wars, or crime, just corporations… and Rollerball. Nonetheless, the film aims to convey that the individual is greater than the game in its conclusion.

The Hindu epic, *The Mahabharath*, narrates the internecine conflict between two ruling clans, the Pandavs, and the Kauravs. One of its principal characters, Duryodhan, a Kaurav, develops a deep hatred for his cousins, the Pandavs. The Pandavs had laughed at Duryodhan's clumsiness, which he saw as a jibe referring to his blind father. This deep-seated hatred prevents Duryodhan from seeing reason and sharing the throne. Because of his stubbornness, he brings about the destruction of his entire clan, the Kauravs.

Duryodhan has a personality complex that interferes with the ability to reason. Most of us brush aside incidents like people laughing at us with an attitude reflected in the statement, 'Rubber glue, back to you.' We could feel some discomfort, but we avoid being bogged down.

Duryodhan was constantly troubled because he depended on artificial props. He wanted to be the sole heir to the throne to feel complete. Duryodhan's enmity with the Pandavs stemmed from an unreasonable competitive attitude, a need to deprive and be one-up. His philosophy reflects what competition should not be. Competing purely to establish

---

18 A remarkable departure from the norm, but one which nonetheless demonstrates that sport is bigger than just a game, is reflected in Dr Vijay Barse's movement in India, slum soccer. The aim of the slum soccer network is reaching out to the Indian homeless using football as a tool for social improvement and empowerment. Visit http://www.slumsoccer.org

relative superiority or inferiority in our lives, as in a game, never leads to a positive conclusion.

We must overcome the spurious license that conditions us to treat life as only a game. Instead, we become more caring when we acknowledge the non-competitive issues in life that require our attention.

*   *   *

We *can* rise above any propaganda that makes us feel whatever we are, or have, is inadequate. One-upmanship and the killer instinct *will* stop affecting us when we change the yardsticks by which we measure our success. The power we feel is tremendous when we focus on doing our best and celebrating personal achievements.

Motivation with an external focus on winning and losing is self-defeating. On the other hand, the motivation that makes you want to better yourself and your situation, leading to *personal* successes, is self-sustaining.

The conventionally accomplished will refuse this version of competition as discouraging. But one must add for our flag-bearers: winning *does* matter. Nobody is attempting to steal your thunder. Nevertheless, common laurels are transient without continuous positive strokes to the psyche.

Despite popular beliefs about winning and losing in the game of life, life is too real to be so lightly discounted. Life is not a game when 95 percent of our population could suffer from put-downs by the remaining five[19]. It is not a game if we feel forced to crave tokens of superior status. It is not a game when innocent children believe they must be better than the Joneses. Further, it is not a game when we look at life based on

---

19 See CNBC's Reporter and Editor Robert Frank's article titled *Who me? A One Percenter* dated 26th July 2012, on the extent of the skew and misconceptions as regards affluence.

trophies acquired instead of cherishing what you have achieved *for the inner you.*

When people say, 'winning is everything,' we should take it to mean—*find success in everything.* We must realize that winning is not a top result with the right mindset. Winning is a by-product. If we focus energy on improving, even in small increments, the outcomes would be outstanding, in some respect or another. We would be able to look back at where we once were and are now with equanimity.

* * *

Do we feel at a competitive disadvantage when we wake up to a challenging environment? Should we fight because of our chosen disagreement (or agreement) or just for superiority? Is there a personal alternative to consider? Is it too hard to believe that an enriched subjective intent can be a successful strategy? What is healthy competition?

Sure, it is hard. Nachiket is also skeptical. But really, the degree of comfort we attain when we let go of relative yardsticks in life is phenomenal. There are other valid and more enduring concepts to live by. Let's ask ourselves, *what constitutes fair competition in which you can win or lose without depriving or feeling deprived?* We see this next.

THE BONA FIDE BATTLE

Section Highlights

- Our dreams must be for things larger than just us while still being incomparably personal and inspiring.
- Actual competition, which gets progressive results, is not from conflict with, or victory over, another person or entity.
- Instead, actual competition measures our 'response-ability' in facing our unique situations.
- We can set our own unique personal benchmarks without seeing ourselves in conflict or competition with others.

- Causative reactions from a subtle core and the person's intent at the time of action, not the action alone, determine if the desired results materialize.
- Effectively competing is all about an ability to create enough options for others to choose from, improving the odds that our choices will bring about the results we desire.
- If our intentions are caring, considerate and helpful, and, we include others in our sense of success, progressive results occur appropriately.

Are the things commonly making us contest incorrect? What is clear to me is that we usually compete for a better world of our own—professional, personal, and social. However, most people conclude that these things are relative and that we must compete for a higher relative position. In addition, many are also in conflict to establish the superiority of their beliefs.

What we believe to be good or bad is not absolute, and many things have a degree of both. What is legal in one country could be illegal in another. Sex workers are legal in Thailand and illegal almost the world over. Similarly, a cancer patient may ingest marijuana legally in some parts of the USA[20]. In an extraordinary case, the Pope pardoned the eating of human flesh by plane-crash victims.

Sometimes the correct thing to do insofar as our employer is concerned might be wrong in the eyes of several others (Imagine being a pro-tobacco lobbyist). *So how do we recognize the conflict to pick? How do we develop the appropriate competitive spirit?*

Ironically, a personal perspective makes the competition we face generic. No single person (or persons) in any frame of time or space

---

20 Two US states, Washington and Colorado, had voted to permit 'recreational' use of marijuana, in contravention of Federal law on the date of publication of the first edition of this book

causes the need to compete. Our struggle is not with another entity but with a situation that is ours and ours alone.

* * *

Winning, without another losing, needs an understanding of internally focused competition. So, let's entirely isolate the person from the situation to get to that. This we will do by first addressing the question: *Why do some competitions and conflicts seem unending or indeterminable, sometimes with unjust, inadequate, or delayed results, even in conclusion?*

I attempt here a pseudo-scientific stab at explaining 'indeterminism' and 'uncertainty' in the consequences of our actions as a precursor to the concept of independent winning. This explanation includes ideas from quantum physics and Einstein's thinking simplistically, having no other basis but speculation. The model can be easily pooh-poohed but does offer an unusual perspective to reflect on.

The figure (Pic. 2—*A Representation of Uncertainty in Creation*) represents action percolating to Creation's building blocks (quanta). These building blocks are at the sub-atomic core of Creation, where time is non-linear. Reactions, consequences, or related external events could be from this core.

Pic 2. A Representation of Uncertainty in Creation

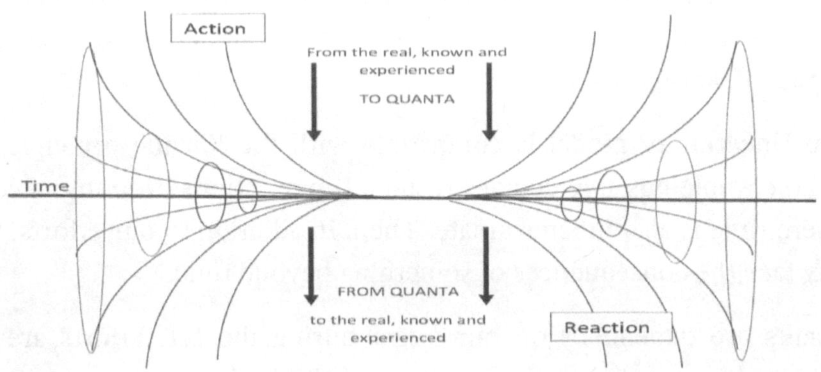

A person could experience reactions to his action in a different time and space. This explanation is not just a leap of faith. We *are* aware that some events happen quite randomly. We attribute them to chance.

Imagine, for example, a narrow escape on a pedestrian crossing. A car almost hits you. Suppose we knew all the relevant details of the vehicle that missed you. The car that almost hit you, and to which you gave a one-finger salute before going your way, was delayed because of a faulty fuel injection system, which would have been rectified a week ago— if the car driver had not fallen ill. Well, you get the drift!

The question is, 'What is chance?' *Is something at an intangible core triggering what we face in the tangible? Are there upward or downward causations between quantum particles and their large configurations, between the subtle and the gross? Is this what chance is? Why you?* We leave the questions begging... *Chance...* hmmm....

Chance is hard to grasp. We do not attribute chance happenings to a detached God, aliens from outer space, or a mad experiment in which we are networked to a reality simulator. Still, conflicts and incidents we experience could have causes elsewhere in the space-time continuum, as suggested in the Uncertainty model.

But no discussion on chance is complete without addressing karma (Yes, we need to go there). Karma is a Hindu and Buddhist belief. Many interpret karma as the underlying principle that makes actions rebound as consequences or results. Actions are both influenced by, and the impact of, karma.

The Uncertainty model is compatible with the Karmic principle. A greater whole possibly decides results. If our actions drop into a core where time is also indeterminate. Then, in addition to our efforts, we may face the consequences of something beyond time.

Results are dependent on our *intent* during the act. Efforts are in themselves neutral, but the intention of the initiator causes a karmic 'load.' When people drop egoistic seeds into the deeper core, they reap inhibited or no rewards, even if the actions seem constructive. But, on the other hand, if the intent is overarching, more caring of bigger concerns, and aimed at helping others, the results are likely to be palpable… somewhere… sometime.

We might look at social competition this way. But what are the explanations for devastating events and challenges that many suffer? Can the trigger for these be explained? More on this a little later.

* * *

It is hard to accept that some struggles we face result from unknown quantum effects, karma, or unfathomable fate. This is primarily because of our awareness of and respect for free will. Free will is alive and well. Here is how we could look at it.

Consider an intelligent divide exists between what we meet and how we meet it. To do this, let us distinguish between Fate and Destiny. Fate is what you meet or encounter, and destiny results from how we confront what we meet[21]. The environment we are in, or face, is fate. And, what we do in it creates destiny.

The doorbell rings, and we are ignorant of who is on the other side of the door. That is fate (what you meet). Whether we choose to open the door or not is destiny (how you meet it). Now a twist: What we do affects the fate of others and how the external world unfolds.

The caller's choice—the destiny he fabricated—was to ring the doorbell, which became our fate—a situation to face. Similarly, when we choose to open the door, this decision becomes the person's fate on the other side of the door.

The final twist: Consider that our actions could create options for others to choose from, and thus we contribute to making the fate we face.

---

21 Swami Chinmayananda (1916-93)

By keeping your light on, a handy doorbell button, and not hanging a 'Do Not Disturb' sign, you created options that allowed the doorbell to be rung. When the person at the door rang the doorbell, he started the options for you to choose whether to open the door, shout 'Get lost!' or sit as quiet as a mouse and wait for the person to go away.

In this example, the action of ringing the doorbell triggered only one set of possible transactions. You could potentially create all the options for others' choices. *Our choices make options from which others choose.* THIS IS THE COMPLETE UNCERTAINTY OR KARMIC CYCLE.

We, in fact, will face a future in whose creation we can (and do) play a significant part. Correspondingly, we are what we are, and where we are, because of the options we presented to others. Today is the result of many options we created, somewhere... sometime... from which others chose— possibilities we may even *be ignorant of or have forgotten making.*

This is what Dharmaraj meant when he said, 'When you create enough options for others to choose from, you can influence their decisions.'

What *are* we competing with, then? We are not competing with one another, as in a game or sport. Instead, people appear to be grappling with each other because of a mad scheme of *civilization.* We believe we are against *one another* when we are only facing our own unique situations.

The real competition is how we dialogue with our fate and create our destiny. Destiny helps our fate turn out to be better and vice-versa. From this point forward, we can construct much of our future and even pre-empt any adverse fate. Leave the rest behind decisively.

* * *

Nachiket saw competition and conflict, the need to win and conquer, as thrust upon him. Dharmaraj attempted to convey to Nachiket that people are worthy of their own successes and do not need to imitate or compare themselves. They need not feel superior or inferior.

Dr. Dharmaraj was trying to ignite this sense in Nachiket, who was, at heart, thinking on a relative plane. Instead, he wanted him to see his position as unique... a situation in which to take ownership. The doctor sought Nachiket to understand that in the ultimate analysis, the circumstances he faced, how he reacted, and what he cared about were his own making.

You should understand that you compete with nothing or no one else. There is nothing relative. We apply effort to better ourselves. This, then, is our bona fide battle.

You would have got a sense of the alternative philosophy on competing proposed. Such an alternative personal philosophy on competition is not selfish. Additionally, it is not about closing eyes to achievement. Instead, the essence of such a perspective aligns with results.

This outlook involves developing a sense of belonging to something larger without the need to be 'superior' relative to others. Our need to be on top of others seems to be a part of the collective mnemonic's tenets. This is also the undoing of living collaboratively as a race.

We find it hard to tolerate other beliefs, leave alone celebrate different schools of thought. However, when we broaden our vision to distinguish between constructive and destructive ideas, unbiased by their origin, we can find the ability to *win* together.

* * *

Your first fundamental principle of the book—a mantra to be embellished in gold in your mind—is '*Meet your fate; make your destiny.*'

We may not be able to choose what we meet. Accept this with as much matter-of-factness as you do the fact you are alive. Drop the relative measures and accept yourself and your situation—right here, right now.

Become genuinely concerned with bettering what concerns you. Show up... and act on your concerns. The rest just happens. Tackle it.

CHAPTER 5

IN - SANITY

'What has happened with me?' Nachiket demanded to know after a few uneventful sessions. These sessions had seemed to be of the usual intensity. However, in hindsight, Dr. Dharmaraj realized that Nachiket had gradually ceased addressing him as divine.

The doctor had thought Nachiket would work his way up to such a question after gradually developing insight. Still, there it was, suddenly. So, the doctor decided it was time for psychoeducation and told Nachiket the truth.

'To be honest, we don't know yet. There is evidence of neurotransmitters being involved. These are chemicals that bridge information from one brain nerve cell to the other. An imbalance of these chemicals in certain areas of the brain causes it to malfunction. So, despite its mental manifestation, it is partly due to a chemical imbalance. The good news is that you are responding to medication.'

'Then what about all I still sense and my suspicions? It seems valid and coherent,' Nachiket asked, puzzled.

'The brain has a funny way of rationalizing,' the doctor explained. 'It thinks in patterns. So even if something strange happens, it forces itself to try and detect a pattern. That is why all you experienced seemed valid.'

'Am I ill?' Nachiket inquired.

'You are not so much ill as confused,' Dharmaraj reassured him. 'It is a combination of factors from physiology, social conditions, stress, and innate sensitivity that trigger such symptoms. Perhaps you are as ill as someone with diabetes or high blood pressure. However, the comparison is not fully accurate. Medication could help, but it may not be the only curative measure.'

"I don't know how to think without my beliefs, perceptions of a different way of communication, and the conclusions I have reached,' declared Nachiket.

'Let's look at these,' said Dr. Dharmaraj. 'Don't debate if the perceptions are real or not. Just ask yourself, are they helpful? Can they help you to live happily and productively with others?' Dharmaraj paused. Nachiket's answer could mean the difference between developing the intent to recover and wallowing in his contorted thinking. The answer came slowly.

'I think...it...could be... But, no, it is not right. Such beliefs do not help in productive and constructive living. However, some of it still seems strangely valid...' Nachiket responded.

Dharmaraj was relieved. Nachiket was seeing a glimmer of reason despite the continuing symptoms. 'The symptoms of this condition influence you. It is normal to feel confused when you couple this with the inherent ambiguity of symbols in the environment, such as language and body language.

'I felt all of Creation was focused on me alone. I felt like I was the center of the Universe. And now everything I sensed is wrong!' exclaimed Nachiket.

'There is success in this, not the apparent failure you perceive.' Dharmaraj said animatedly. 'It will take some time, but let me assure you, those who have gone through this condition and recovered are in many ways better equipped now. It may seem clichéd, but you will see that tough times don't last. Tough people do!'

'But all that understanding...the feeling people communicate in radical ways...,' said Nachiket.

'For many, such a communication style is inherent,' Dr. Dharmaraj explained. 'Some others even deliberately complicate interaction using it. Both spurious and valid communication cues do exist.

Many people find it challenging to differentiate spurious alerts from valid ones. The cues are sometimes ambiguous and hard to decipher. Moreover, for some, the signals may seem hostile and aggressive instead of collaborative when first perceived.

You did not see such patterns earlier. You were too self-absorbed. Now that you have awakened and become aware, you will be a better judge of what is valid and what is not. You can relearn trust.'

'When I look back at what happened to me, I see a progression of suspicions and doubts,' agreed Nachiket. 'I still don't see how I will fit in with other people.'

'Typically, we fail to notice the things that will help us get along in society because of our internal focus. Experts claim that only seven percent of what is understood depends on the explicitly stated. Instead, we base a substantial portion of our understanding on tone and visual cues such as body language. When you perceive this or interact with an aggressive individual, you might feel ill-equipped.

However, if you passionately believe in a growing personal purpose, you will not be intimidated. Instead, you will be proactive and take the learning life offers. Everything, including the unusual patterns, will be grist to your mill.' Dr. Dharmaraj was trying hard to make the transition easier.

'But many others seem "awake" to these aspects of Creation much before me.' Nachiket air-quoted, sounding miffed. 'My parents never taught me all this. Isn't this unfair?'

'Honestly, Nachiket,' said the doctor, 'there is nothing to teach. Nobody, your parents included, can force awareness. These aspects are very personal and learned by observation.'

'When I see the lost time, I feel I can never make up. My schoolmates are better placed than I am. I could have lost the race,' said Nachiket, resorting once again to relative measures.

Dharmaraj reminded him, 'Again, why do you feel you should be measured by the success of others? You have unique learning that is yours and yours alone. We will talk about this next time.

Relax. Review your notes. Just think of the time lost as a sabbatical in which you were learning something special. We spoke a little about personally unique goals. We will talk more on this the next time.'

This was a sign of a breakthrough, which the doctor had been waiting for. Nachiket had begun to see that the delusional patterns he had experienced could be wrong. The medications were acting well, the hallucinations were receding, and he was gaining more focus. Nevertheless, a successful conclusion could still be far away.

The doctor added a mild anti-depressant to his prescription, anticipating adverse feelings Nachiket might have as he gained insight. The doctor also told the parents to encourage conversation and give Nachiket small, achievable, everyday tasks around the house.

THE SURROGATE SENSE

Section Highlights

- Some people ascribe strange connectivity or meaning to sensory trivia in their environment.
- In addition, 'synchronicity' can mystify some people. Synchronicity is an 'acausal connecting principle' that Carl Jung claimed bridges the dream and the real world.

- The connectivity and overlaid meaning are due to the brain's tendency to fabricate coherence even in the random.
- We can view any disembodied cues we experience as extended metaphors of early trauma presented for us to resolve.
- Knowing the brain's tendency to fit trivial stimuli into a surrogate sense can help us demystify much of our environment.

The second problem that affects the psyche is faulty cues from the collective mnemonic. The collective mnemonic, though unintelligent, seems to have enough artistic sense to suggest imaginary connections. It pushes the mind to derive meanings in random stimuli, attempting to make sense of miscellaneous symbols.

The arrangements perceived may have harmless artistic sense and appeal, like viewing patterns in a kaleidoscope. People with a creative bent of mind can appreciate the designs around them. But, on the other hand, some others may be disturbed and distracted.

A few impart connectivity to the random that is neither rational nor artistic. The arrangements could appear to judge, challenge, or dominate.

Some of us may wonder, 'What *is* this?' Spurious negative connectivity, when experienced, can cause havoc when we don't have plausible explanations for the phenomenon.

We know that language is a great gift, and the mind is a beautiful instrument. However, the mind's ability to detect patterns and derive meaning sometimes acts against us. When the detections of the mind are deviant, it could lead to strange conclusions, out-of-sync with a larger context.

Some aspects—disembodied stimuli, body language, double entendre, chance happenings, and coincidences that people sometimes experience— may confuse us.

The 'disorienters' show up because introspection combines with an overactive imagination, a common trait of schizophrenia. Such aspects force personal reactions bordering on superstition.

We will add demystifying understanding in this chapter. This understanding would help rise above confusing 'disorienters.' You will see how bizarre the world of the flawed collective mnemonic can get. Be cautioned; we will walk a thin line between the rational and the irrational.

* * *

What sets about schizophrenia? How can one prepare to face surreal challenges? As discussed earlier—different environments, foreign lands, cultures, social paradigms, or new relationships are a part of life. Any new reality could challenge our comfortable cocoon of explanations.

Some attempt a way back using only known rules and logic, especially if they go by theory. We try to understand any novel experiences using theoretical learning alone. Some, like Nachiket, reach spurious conclusions, as what they know cannot explain what they perceive.

The collective mnemonic in a person's psyche may cause stressful inner conflict. Issues like the erstwhile Cold War, the fear of God, spirits, nuclear oblivion, or a need to rebel against authority are some conflicts an afflicted person could feel entangled in. Such conflicts can be a foundation for some bizarre types of connectivity and communication.

For example, they may cause a sensitive individual to connect various published articles and believe an elaborate conspiracy exists. The Hollywood movie, *A Beautiful Mind* portrays this. The film is based, even if loosely, on the true story of American Nobel laureate John Nash, a person afflicted with schizophrenia[22]. It shows him looking for coded messages to spies in news articles. Similarly, a deeply religious individual could infer divine messages from the daily newspaper.

---

22 Nasar, Sylvia. *A Beautiful Mind*. Simon & Schuster Paperbacks, print.

The overly sensitive often create an artificial and delusional framework of explanations for their unusual perceptions. Stressed 'normal' persons may also see peculiar meanings in the environment.

For example, when stressed, the not-so-vulnerable could be sensitive to events such as a black cat crossing their path. This is not alarming when it does not influence significant decisions. However, when a person relies on a kind of surrogate sense for decisions, it causes behavior that seems insane or eccentric.

How does this happen? I ask you to consider that the brain's frontal lobe could automatically link random experiences and events in a person's vicinity[23]. The brain tends to link up everything in the vicinity to whatever is the mind's concern. The afflicted individual lives with strange connectivity, imaginatively associating the environment, the corporal, and the mental.

For some, these connections are deviant. A simple example: The entry of a person named Roger into a room could cause a stressed and sensitive individual to make an abnormal connection. Pressed for time, he immediately approves a proposal under discussion. He does this because 'Roger' is military jargon for 'Okay,' and not because of the contextual merit of the proposal.

The mind can also derive surrogate meaning lacking common reason in other ways. For example, there is strange rationality during dreaming where the nonsensical seems sensible. During REM (Rapid Eye Movement) sleep, the stage when we dream, the frontal lobe does what it is best at doing: giving coherence to randomness. This leads to the dream's apparent continuity, keeping the dreamer dreaming and asleep.

However, imparting dream-like associations and inferences to random happenings in a waking state is peculiar. To help you see what this

---

23 Some research points to the limbic cortex and not the frontal lobe as the
    place from which the most primal and random connectivity could emerge.

means, trace back a random train of thought when awake. A chain of thinking could end in topics far removed from its trigger.

For example, an advertising billboard for shoes reminds you that you left in a hurry and did not polish your shoes, despite a business meeting. Then, you think of the business proposal you made for the meeting last night and your child's homework. Finally, you recall that you could lend no help to your child because of the business proposal you had to make.

The distinction between a regular chain of thinking and what is an odd chain is the mix-up of its perceived intent. An afflicted person could interpret his failure to help the child as *the* insinuation of the advertisement.

A phenomenon along similar lines is *synchronicity*. Due to its esoteric nature, synchronicity is an occurrence with minimal formal research. In its vanilla form, synchronicity is merely a noticeable coincidence. Carl C Jung speculated that synchronicity is an 'acausal connecting principle' between dreams and the real world.

Jung suggested one should find the common meaning of such simultaneous internal and external events [coincidences]. We need not look for a magical relationship as they did in medieval times.

Dr. Remo Roth, a psychologist in Zurich, who provides an intriguing collection of information on a German website, has this to say about Jung and synchronicity in an English translation of his site[24].

Jung cites in his letters [Jung, 1973, p. 395] an occurrence that is an impressive example of synchronicity: 'For instance, I walk with a woman patient in the woods. She tells me about the first dream in her life that had made an everlasting impression upon her. She dreamt of a spectral fox descending the stairs in her parental home. At this moment, a real fox comes out of the trees about forty yards away and

---

24 www.psychovision.ch (Was available at the time of publishing the first
    edition)

pads on the path ahead of us for several minutes. The animal behaves like a partner in the human situation.'

According to Jung, it would be wrong and extremely dangerous to see a causal relationship between the two occurrences and say that one event was the cause of the other. That would be nothing but a relapse to the magical-causal thinking of the middle-ages. So instead, we must accept that the two occurrences are not causally connected but have only an associative meaning.

This means that we must extract the implication of the symbol 'fox' to interpret this synchronicity. He suggests this would somehow purport that the patient, metaphorically speaking, should be led much more by her 'inner fox.' The message is that she must recover the instinctive cleverness [ingenuity] she had replaced with her intellectual point of view.

Jung's interpretation is a helpful conclusion. There is an implicit assumption in the example that people experience synchronicity without seeing it as hostile or isolating. Persons with schizophrenia, however, could perceive such instances as malicious.

Suppose an afflicted or ordinary person cannot interpret these instances as helpful aids. Then, in the interest of sanity, it is better not to read any meaning into them at all. There is no reason to believe there is meaning in the event or that it has a context pertinent to the individual. It is what it is—an experience of coincidence. The event is open to multiple interpretations. This could lead to many a wild fox, wild goose chase!

When under stress, a person may interpret spontaneous activity in the environment as connected to personal situations, actions, or thoughts. The figure shows that the connection can be harmless and uncomplicated (Pic. 3—*Connectivity: An Example*). This scenario captures the essence of the strange connectivity between a person and his surroundings. It is an example of how people may read fanciful meanings into everyday situations.

Pic 3. Connectivity: An Example

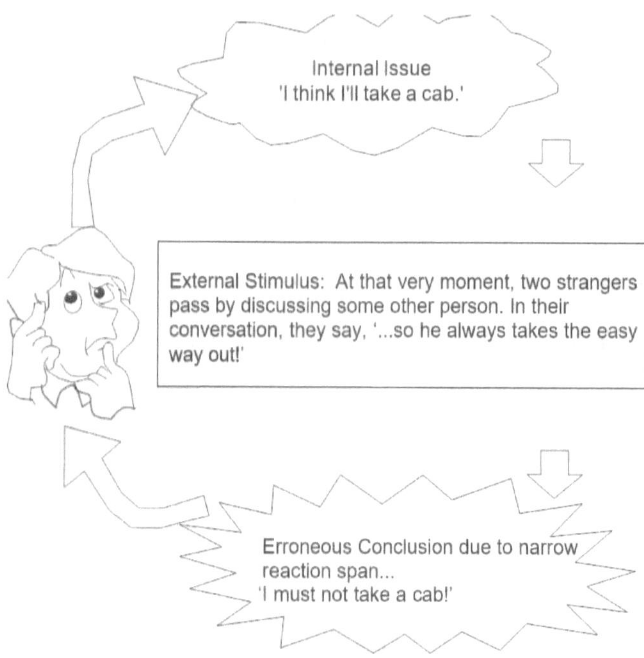

Additionally, this illustrates the mind's tendency to be influenced by the immediate vicinity rather than that which is contextual (in a more relevant time and scope). The reference span for decisions is localized, happens in the now, and deviates from a larger meaningful context.

Because of such 'localization,' some afflicted also experience *spatial stimuli*. These are stimuli of insentient objects in the person's vicinity. A person reads abnormal meaning into the physical arrangements of the things in the environment.

He may impart an underlying meaning to innocuous placements of objects surrounding him. Usually, individuals experience ease or unease and consequently confer an inner message to these arrangements.

An example of such an influence is when a person comes across a street name and infers it to be a personalized message. More specifically, the street name Mahatma Gandhi Road may be interpreted as criticizing the person for being martyrlike.

Since this form of connectivity links insentient objects and uses them for deriving overlaid messages and direction, they can be termed *spatial influencers*.

We can extend this kind of odd interpretation of the mind into an area where theoretical knowledge remains sketchy and speculative as it is with the other forms of connectivity discussed. This different form of connectivity is from body reflexes or motor symbolism, which we discussed earlier in Chapter 1 in the Section *Eclectic Esperanto*.

Recall LAD (Language Acquisition Device) and UG (Universal Grammar) of Chomsky. We could hazard that some bodily reflexes originate from a corporal blueprint imprinted in our lineage. The body language arising from this blueprint is specific to a culture or race. Some of it occurs automatically in toddlers and adults yet to become aware of their bodies.

Most interpretations of the cues encountered have an element of subjectivity. Therefore, collectively endorsed interpretations vary from environment to environment, differing among social groups, cultures, geographic areas, languages, etc. Such connectivity could influence decisions, even though it seems irrational.

An example of a physical, social cue is flicking the thumb against the pointing finger, palm facing inwards. This gesture indicates apathy for the other person while otherwise appearing interested.

More examples of inventive meanings among the various possible genres of connectivity attributable to the collective mnemonic are postulated in Table 2 - *Examples of Connectivity in Various Genres*.

The tricky aspect is that several people often balance this surrogate sense and deal rationally. This makes them appear normal, but they tend to succumb to this spurious logic when under stress.

Table 2. Examples of Connectivity in Various Genres

Connectivity Genre	Connectivity Example with Speculated or Derived Meaning
Tradition	Associating footwear with insult and disrespect
Superstition	Believing a sneeze is a bad omen
Word Play	Conjuring an alternative meaning (e.g., Paris as 'Pair Is') to help the person act during a deadlocked transaction. Or extending the word 'umbrella' to mean an overarching protective psychic shroud
Synchronicity	Using dream-like associations, *déja vu*, or coincidences to make decisions. e.g., seeing personal relevance in the sudden appearance of a cat
Spatial Influencers	Deriving personal meaning from innocuous objects. e.g., Seeing a traffic signpost declaring a road as one-way as a reference to one's own standing in a matter. Or, see a tuning fork on top of a document as metaphorically related to its harmonious appeal.
Corporal Symbolism	Displaying the palm facing outwards with thumb and fingers outstretched to form a 'Y,' expressing a desire to understand and influence the situation
Metaphorical	Perceiving disembodied criticism even when there is none, reflecting insecurity from early childhood pressures to excel

Unfortunately, we cannot explain *why* the mind tends towards such vagueness in its perceptions. Some of it is residual in us, caused by our journey originating in savage beginnings to today's human societies.

The cave dwellers had no need to think beyond immediate time and space. Could the lack of advanced symbolic tools like language have caused early humans to rely on bodily cues?

Some primal tendencies carried over to the present through our lineage may inhibit fresh perspectives today.

***

Most such cues appear to have a conjured 'form.' Some people hence believe there is a purpose – that the signals cause an underlying psychic reaction.

Reflect on the possible consequences of applying this misinterpretation and signaling in groups such as families, cults, corporate boardrooms, or governments. The implications are spine-tingling. *Do some people say one thing and do another with impunity because of an extended license from the collective mnemonic? Are they manipulating others through the collective mnemonic? Are such people driving society?* These were among Nachiket's fears, brought to a head by his sensitivity.

I argue that through imitation over generations, a subscribing group has etched such cues in the mnemonic. Such a common (or, as put forward, uncommon) understanding of cues continues to pass down generations.

Further, some people introduce such cues deliberately to intimidate others in interactions. They seem esoterically aware and knowledgeable about using this surrogate sense. It could be an essential survival skill in the context of their group.

'Aware' individuals use and misuse their awareness, despite a lack of relevance to the context. Usually, such 'aware' people attempt to adjust the power balance using such cues. This is why sensitive individuals, at the receiving end, perceive hostility in the public use of such signals instead of seeing it as just another form of transaction or communication.

***

Recall the collective mnemonic, in addition to passing on flawed social impressions, also houses an illiterate side of Nature. From this side of Nature springs forth corrupt connections of symbols sensed by the afflicted. Interpretations of such connectivity by them are inventive, speculative, and idiosyncratic.

People, egged on by popular superstitions and uncertainty in the sciences, may ascribe magical or religious explanations for the odd cues, coincidences, and serendipity experienced. Unfortunately, they seem only conjured because the collective mnemonic has an unknown—or at best, unconfirmed—basis.

We must appreciate that there will be a lack of context and irrationality in the trivia we face. Hence, we must avoid trying to make 'logic' out of every bit of such sensory trivia, especially when it provokes hostile or aggressive reactions and behavior.

Some of the more personal manifestations of cues (such as the metaphorical kind) may exist to point each of us to our singular fulfillment and are to be interpreted positively. For example, suppose some manifestations or cues tell us to do harm. In that case, we can understand in them a metaphor that one is being unforgiving.

We need not feel taken aback or prompted to hurt ourselves or others. Instead, we can let the cues play through helpfully, seeing metaphors that teach us in them. We can choose to be contextual and not confusingly abstract or harmful.

As implied at the chapter's outset, the collective mnemonic can be enjoyably progressive when its cues are artistic, pure, and nurturing. We should be detached and positive in our interpretations and responses when it is not.

FROM NUISANCE TO SENSE

Section Highlights

- Some afflicted people display a sense of 'psychotic grandiosity' and believe they have super-human or extra-sensory powers.

- Some could also believe that changing the arrangements of objects in their vicinity, like poking pins into a voodoo doll, can affect remote events.
- Such beliefs are part of the flawed collective mnemonic, suggesting a hidden order and mystical connections in otherwise inane events.
- The best way to approach the second problem of flawed cues is to treat them as inert signals and consciously construct our efforts around the real and meaningful context.
- We need not cave in or respond with hostility but instead be proactive in countering the cues, moving on, and adding any signals we encounter to our experience.

A sense of extreme isolation and introversion could cause grandiose delusions of personal power—termed 'psychotic-grandiosity' in psychiatry. Psychotic grandiosity is often one of the symptoms of schizophrenia. The term refers to a tendency to become obsessively *self-absorbed*.

Some persons acquire an inflated notion of their own importance and ability to influence. The person could have an exaggerated sense of ability and ownership of everything around him. For example, the person may feel entitled to claim a random passing car as his own.

Such self-centered feelings of being one with everything else may be pleasant if it is positive, filled with joy, yet not harmful or addictive! But, most affected individuals believe they are of Universal importance in an unhealthy or unproductive fashion.

Megalomania and distorted sensations of power could lead to awkward acts on one end, right on to destructive behavior on the other.

Recall Nachiket's feelings of having special powers. Many similar delusions, such as a belief that one is bestowed with total discretion over others, or that of being a divine dispenser of justice, could even be dangerous.

There are subtler manifestations of this kind of grandiosity. A person could see an extraordinary ability in himself to affect larger happenings by arranging his immediate environment. For example, he believes that placing his pen over a document influences events related to that document.

An afflicted person carries out such arrangements with obsessive fervor and a devious paranoid agenda. In addition, the person is likely to believe in a supernatural power to influence— such as having the ability to inflict pain by poking pins in a voodoo doll.

Much of our conditioning in religion and other beliefs from our upbringing often tell us we are divine to help build self-esteem. They tell us we are created in the image of God. Or, in some cases, we *are* God. Many feel short-changed if anything suggests that they are perpetually unfinished ideas or constant works-in-progress.

They, therefore, seek a sense of completion and gravitate towards anything that bolsters this belief. Psychotic grandiosity may be fallout from such presumptions of godliness housed in the collective mnemonic.

* * *

In addition to the incidence of spurious cues, the afflicted individual could display a propensity toward grandiose psychotic displays. Combined with hallucinations and delusions, it could prompt superstitious or irrational behavior.

There is no clear explanation for why this happens. Given our limited scientific and human ability, we cannot classify this deeper sensing. Only pseudo-scientific or mystical attempts to set right the uneasiness seem to exist currently.

All the person experiences in these moments may be unease (or sudden ease) at a possible symbolic pattern, a gesture, a phrase, or a physical arrangement. People react instinctively, but the reactions may defy explanations.

The danger is that an individual may read hostility or aggression, often mistakenly, and then react similarly. Alternatively, some people, especially when afflicted, could become diffident or unresponsive, as in the case of Nachiket.

* * *

Jung's crucial observation regarding synchronicity reveals the crux of contending with the various kinds of connectivity discussed. Jung's conclusion that such events are 'acausal' is vital. This observation applies to all forms of random connectivity.

We cannot impart harmful meaning or other hostile 'causal' attributes to the cues resulting from connectivity. Instead, we must realize that the several forms of the surrogate sense are manifestations of an illiterate but 'symbolic' nature (the collective mnemonic) mimicking intelligence.

Sometimes, the cues may need to be seen as allegorical reminders. They exist to correct something in us that has not entirely crystallized to become personal learning.

* * *

How do we manage such a surrogate sense and consequent displays of connectivity thrown up by the collective mnemonic? We must first become conscious of such a deviant tendency in others and ourselves. We can then respond rationally to the use or misuse of such cues and factors by others.

It is best to ignore the manifestations, as they may derail us from the rational. We need not simply try to grab at straws of sense. We also don't have to get defensive or carried away in the face of such spurious presumptions presented by the collective mnemonic.

We can understand and extend Jung's interpretation of synchronicity to other forms of connectivity. This means we should only view the cues as *inert signals* rather than causative forces. Then, if required, we can respond with a neutralizing retort to counter the event or action that triggered the momentary unease. This is a reassuring rejoinder, which contributes to personal poise.

The four-step response that I advise for us to remain poised when you feel dragged into such connectivity are:

1. COUNTER the cue when you sense it and cannot ignore it by doing something frivolous, like copying it or performing a redundant action. For example, when you feel uneasy with someone flipping a palm in your face, steeple your fingers facing the instigator. Your response need not make sense but acknowledges the invasive action to put you back on par. Use *any* retort: verbal, mental, or physical, consciously. Responding helps you go on with poise in the interaction.

2. FOCUS on the more significant real issue or context and ignore or negate attempts of those who use such cues to intimidate, confuse or disrupt interactions. When discussing any topic, stick to the context despite distractions such as subconscious asides, disembodied influencers, double-entendres, odd gestures, or intimidatory posturing. Don't allow such influences to strong-arm or derail your focus on the context.

3. MOVE on in time to new transactions and deliberately get beyond the cues to avoid harmful or confusing impressions. This means stop returning to the signal, take the learning it offers, brush it off, and leave it in the past. Move on.

4. ADD any new cues you come across to your mental list to be better prepared and more proactive the next time you encounter them.

As pointed out almost *ad nauseam*, we must remain contextual in our interactions. We can react immediately to this odd sensing with a rational, proactive response. Otherwise, one may become uneasy; from feeling that one has not done enough, lacks a critical skill, or has inadequate knowledge. Therefore, I suggest you mentally counter the experience of cues using the insights and techniques discussed.

The next best thing to total avoidance, which may be impossible, is to distance yourself. Now that you have explanations on how we could end up erroneously perceiving connectivity, you can be detached enough to respond proactively. Again, constructively collaborating is a wiser response than being aggressive or timid. Learn to ignore the surreal or harmful and keep a level head focused on the context.

If it turns out that you have a better explanation, such as homespun wisdom from your peer group, please adopt it. Use whatever helps you stay on an even keel.

In conclusion, you can try to understand and interpret the cues as virtual coaches, not negative manifestations. Like any coach, they can sometimes seem taxing. But, with an open mind and a reflective disposition, you can analyze, *befriend* and transact using the cues as helpful aids in communication.

One can easily contest what this chapter states, for its lack of backing from academic research, and term it a speculative surmise. Yes, I have drawn these conclusions of mystifying social phenomena only from personal observation. But whether proved factual or merely conjecture restricted in its scope, I intend to help.

By providing a broader explanation for the practical quirks, I hope to prevent as many people as possible from spiraling down into a mental affliction. Furthermore, to the greatest feasible extent, I aim to ensure that people are better equipped than I was to face some peculiarities they may come across.

Whether one is aware or not, flaws in the collective mnemonic, and consequently its cues, may exist. It could be time to know how to face it. If you sense its manifestations, you have seen such an underlying influencer. If you do not, don't be concerned. They are palpable to some only when under excessive stress.

Let us now look at another way of getting equipped to face the social maelstrom—addressing the third problem pointed out in Part 1—the consequences of civilization's *virtual scorecard*.

CHAPTER 6

DESIRE

'Doctor, I think I know what I have to do,' said Nachiket with new bravado at the session's outset. 'I can talk to people and become involved in politics. I think I can make a difference and even become President if I put my mind to it. That is how I can make up for lost time and have people respect me.'

Dharmaraj immediately read the signs. Nachiket was overreacting to compensate for what he saw as his failure. The doctor sensed that he had to approach the issue differently instead of using plain talk.

'I am pleased with your confidence, Nachiket,' he said. 'You can focus on the immediate next steps first. You must relax, get back to having fun with the family, go back to school, or... say... pick up a nice hobby.'

Nachiket held up his hands frustratedly. 'Look at me—how will anybody believe I am normal? I need accomplishments to wash away my past.'

Dharmaraj quoted again: 'If your happiness depends on what somebody else does, you have a problem. You should realize that if success depends on the perceptions of others, you will feel limited in whatever you achieve. There will be a tendency to underplay yourself when you only use such a yardstick.

What you have experienced is a setback. Just learn from it. Realize that you are a unique individual whose only mission in life is to get better in some manner, unrelated to any victory over anything or anyone else.'

Nachiket was blustering once again. 'But when I see the achievements of others, I feel small. I feel handicapped. I have been thinking how I can measure up to be a social success.'

'True success is to better yourself,' Dharmaraj reassured Nachiket. 'If you find the position of another inspiring, pursue that goal. However, if you do not feel inspired and only inadequate or envious, it may be time to realize that goal is not yours. You have a unique destination. Be patient; you will find your calling as you learn increasingly about your capabilities.'

'I have lost so much time. Look at people like Bill Gates. He makes a million every few minutes.' Nachiket was having a tough time giving up comparative measures.

'As long as you rely on comparisons for your sense of achievement, all you do will seem insufficient,' the doctor pointed out. 'Why not focus on getting better and better instead?'

'But everything I want to do costs money,' declared Nachiket. 'Nobody cares if you are useful or not, better or worse, if you have money. So don't you think money is a worthwhile goal?'

'Money is important, but it is not everything,' Dharmaraj responded. 'What is more important is developing faith in your ability to improve, regardless of your situation. There will be a tremendous surge in confidence if you work towards this personal security. Work on your ability to make money, not a quantum of money itself. Money becomes an automatic consequence of your capability and the value you offer.'

'Doctor, people make money without being capable, by unfair and unreasonable means. I have lost a lot of ground. How do I be reasonable and still make money?' said a worried Nachiket.

'You have not lost ground. On the contrary, you have gained insight.' The doctor reminded Nachiket. 'This is more than what several *ordinary* people can claim. Many people go blindly about their lives and are shocked out of their wits at misfortune. However, you avoid any adverse impact by having the right intent. You can set the intention to achieve what you want without feeling affected by the ups and downs in the process.'

'How can this intent endure?' Nachiketh asked. 'It seems such a huge ask, given my lost time.'

'Think about what you will do in small steps of achievement, and revel in these. The big ones come to those who have the humility to appreciate the little results. Money is essential, but it is a consequence of your focus and cannot be its cause. Your primary need should be absolute betterment. Focus on getting better holistically instead of dwelling on any material shortcomings.

'What about the lack of parity in our starting points?' Nachiket asked. 'Some will be at an advantage, correct?'

'They are where they are because of whatever they need to learn and heal in their lives. Some of us need to learn more and some less.' The doctor proposed.

'Isn't my past also a lesson?' Finally, Nachiket caught the thin line between dwelling in the past and progressing from it.

'Surely!' exclaimed the doctor. 'We do not recognize this readily because most of us have not looked at our past squarely. It just happened. We cannot distance ourselves from the events, so we cannot see the lessons.'

'Is there a way to realize these lessons now?' asked Nachiket.

'There is an exercise that would help you to align yourself. It involves writing out the past; looking at it with the perspective you gained in the intervening time. Let us discuss this...'

The doctor taught Nachiket a practice to help him come to terms with his past[25].

---

25 See RI 2 *"The Archived Anxiety"* at the end of book under Recovery Instruments

Dr. Dharmaraj was sure Nachiket was on the right track as he had begun to hope in real terms. Nachiket had become concerned about worldly achievements, even if he was overreaching. The doctor advised the parents to encourage Nachiket's real needs and reassure him that everything could be right again.

Nachiket also had to accept taking the necessary medication. He should treat medication as assistance by science to which he need not attach any stigma.

HAND-BRAKES OFF?

Section Highlights

- The primary repercussions of society's virtual scorecard are being envious of others and/or being dissatisfied with our self-appraisal.
- We can ascertain the validity of our goals and desires by classifying them into rational needs or irrational wants.
- For our discussions, fulfilling a need typically does not upset anyone, including oneself, but fulfilling a want is likely to disturb others or result in an imbalanced self.
- When a desire or a dream is based on comparisons and disconnected from inspiration, it can be a brake on effective functioning and progress.
- When we recognize 'unworthiness' as a blessing that approves us to not have that which does not belong to us, we get clarity on the things we need and are 'worthy' of.
- We must realize that each one of us is so unique that nothing and no one was, is, or will ever be just like us.

The third issue affecting Nachiket and contributing to his schizophrenic condition is civilization's *virtual scorecard*. This is a comparative standard based on pre-existing social measures of success. However, the desire to measure up in such social scoring is sometimes misplaced. This desire is misplaced when only convincing victories support our self-worth.

How can we be purposeful, in a uniquely personal fashion, in the face of *any* social scrutiny or scoring? Dr. Dharmaraj posited that an individual can realize a unique, non-relative, and enduring private purpose.

It happens when we consciously manage constraints such as greed, desire, and selfishness. Some feel these aid achievements, but they can become mental brakes that kill performance. They can retard sustained effort.

We will explore two specific brakes that result from keeping social scores. Although they may help induce effort, I see these as retarding our progress. These brakes trigger a wide range of impairments. They prevent the recognition of independent personal successes. The brakes are a part of the disposition that contributed to the onset of mental health issues with Nachiket.

Once we release these brakes, we can become comfortable with our life's purpose. We develop our own set of standards, deliver our personal best, and appreciate the grace of life.

* * *

The first emotional brake to explore is envy. The harmful thinking that first leads to extreme introspection, some dark phases, and perhaps schizophrenia, could have roots in envy or jealousy.

Envy is seeded in a false feeling of inadequacy caused by misplaced desires. It may have sentenced some people to feel that they are less than what others are, despite having their own achievements. The envious person feels his achievements cannot measure up to the expectations of the world or his own expectations of himself. Popular standards override our ability to be satisfied with 'average' personal achievement.

Adopting comparative standards of success throws even regular people into extreme, sometimes damaging, introspection. Even capable people are often envious. This kind of introspection, prompted by comparisons, can even lead to a mental crisis.

One cannot appreciate the efforts applied or emulate excellence when one is envious. Envy is not a result of disagreement with an idea or event. We could understand that merit or popularity exists in the envied person's success. Still, another person's success may be impossible to accept due to our personal anxieties.

The hidden agenda of envy asks, *what does that person have that I cannot deliver, given the same circumstances and opportunity?*

Envy can also change in intensity as a reaction to the degree of others' successes. When another person gets a better car, envy might crop up. When this individual acquires a second car, this feeling could become more intense, especially when one desires a similar vehicle. The timing or probability of getting the car we want seems unfavorable, triggering harmful feelings.

It is difficult to sense personal success when we feel what we do is less rewarding than what others have succeeded at. This, in fact, is most of the popularly coveted things. Hence, it is essential to disconnect our sense of achievement from comparative measures and connect it to inner well-being.

* * *

Why do we compare ourselves to others and sometimes end up feeling inadequate? Why can we not accept or celebrate the success of those we dislike? That then is the problem. The best way to tackle this is to realize that the other person's achievements have nothing to do with our dreams except when they are an inspiration.

When is envious desire inspiring, and when is it counter-productive? A question that helps add clarity is, 'Will the fulfillment of the desire *cater to a necessity or not?'* Of course, food, clothing, and shelter are necessities.

In the early days of humankind, the cave dweller had to hunt and kill game to feed his family. Hunting was a necessity, as cultivating crops was unknown. However, there is one thing that sets such killing apart. The basic survival needs—food, clothing, and shelter— required some action, killing animals being one such action. Survival needed killing. This separates it from pointless slaughter.

We could make a similar distinction between right and wrong, responsible and irresponsible, appropriate and wishful desires, and other such dichotomies by realizing what is valid for us.

Validation comes from telling *needs* and *wants* apart. Needing is a rational desire. Wanting, as defined for our discussion, is an irrational one. A 'need' is constructive and something that cannot be done without. It is a rational desire. On the other hand, a' want' is usually irrational and adds to personal imbalance.

Your need is a consuming desire to get something for yourself. Your want is a consuming desire to get something someone else has (or deprive someone). It could also be a completely irrational obsession. Want is always for something extra and usually exceeds a person's needs.

Some of our wants masquerade as needs. Such desires may require fulfillment, for they seem to be a prerequisite to our larger goals. For example, a mobile phone is a vital tool for everyone. However, my goal of doing business with leading personalities could force me to consider not just *a* mobile phone but also a top-of-the-line model. Is this a need or a want?

Now, what happens when I cannot get this phone and a sneaky, no-good, slimy rival, whom I dislike intensely, already has one? Since we live in a society, someone would already have what we desire before we get it (assuming we ever do).

On the other hand, people lack necessities when they don't even have what is needed. They are not self-sufficient. They are trying to fill in something missing, without which their life is incomplete. It is part of their requirement, dream, and vision.

So, is the desire for a top-of-the-line model cell phone a need or a want? Is Nachiket's desire to be President a need or a want? Questions of this kind can be answered only with a personal perspective and assimilating the following explanation.

We can try to see our desires in the right light by considering a statement and some concepts based on the *Life 101* series by John-Rogers (aka Roger D Hinkins)[26] and Peter McWilliams (1949–2000)[27]. They coined the phrase, 'We can get anything we want, but we cannot get everything we want.' Reword that into— 'We can get anything we need, but we cannot get everything we want[28].'

An unusual understanding is that we must accept some 'unworthiness' (Yes, unworthiness!). Unworthiness realizes that some things are not structured to come to us. This unworthiness is supportive if we unlink the semantic baggage the word typically carries. This allows us to be without anything not earmarked as ours.

We must view this unworthiness as a friend, just as we do worthiness. These two feelings keep us on the path to what is truly ours—our own dreams and not somebody else's. Unworthiness is the friend that says, 'Your proper path is not this way.' Our unworthiness does not disconnect from purpose but is a compass indicating a path to our specific success.

The sense of not being on track (being unworthy) leads to discovering what you can enjoy and accomplish (what you are worthy of). Dr.

---

26 Roger Delano Hinkins, known and published as John-Rogers, is an American author and public speaker
27 Peter Alexander McWilliams was an American self-help author
28 McWilliams, Peter: *Do It! Let's Get Off Our Buts*. Atlantic Books, 1998

Dharmaraj, in his dialogues, tried to transform the confusing feelings of worthiness and unworthiness that Nachiket was experiencing into a constructive and usable force.

Indoctrination by social standards of success, many of which are housed in the collective mnemonic, can prevent us from accepting this. Our ego refuses unworthiness due to its perceived connotations. It gives rise to feelings of being psychologically small.

Nevertheless, when we see it as a guiding force, taking us towards our own singular fulfillment, we will feel comfortable with it.

I believe we misinterpret unworthiness and express it as envy. If whatever is desired is truly our path, we would feel inspired, not abrasive and envious. Whether we consider the envied person deserving or otherwise does not matter. The result inspires us.

Attaching aspirations to some independent dimension, de-linked from the envied entity, would release tremendous energy for effort and, hence, a separate success.

We need to realize we are not doing what we do just to be better than someone else. Instead, we do what we do to better what concerns us. With this realization, we remain unaffected by the *taunting* of others and the *flaunting* of incomparable achievements.

When we grant that we are free to live our own independent lives, we will no longer have desires conditioned by others. Instead, we develop the capacity to appreciate our achievements and those of others without comparing. And... even as we appreciate, we aspire to only acquire what inspires!

* * *

You are a distinct being who has never existed before and never will exist again. You are an association of atoms unlike any that was or will ever be. You are an absolute fact in the scheme of Creation. No person, no twin, no clone, is precisely like you.

You could get volumes of comparisons on your looks, attitudes, and skills, with things real and fictional. Still, nothing compares to you and your life. When we realize our uniqueness, we also get to appreciate the uniqueness of others.

Dharmaraj sought to highlight this point for Nachiket. We need never compare ourselves and our situation with anyone, whatever our reality package's pluses and minuses.

This is the second key outlook of the book for us[29]: *Realize your absolute, non-relative, and unique standing.* Emblazon this too in your mind.

We had a look at desire on an emotional plane in this section. In the next section, we look at the physical plane of wealth and luxury.

THE WORRY OF WEALTH

Section Highlights

- Uneven distribution of wealth and the desire to possess more may be social mechanisms that ensure continued investment in value creation.
- Wealth is a consequence of approval and not a cause. One cannot 'buy' genuine approval.
- After a certain basic threshold, enough and more are a state of mind, not the material.
- We can cherish out-of-reach chance pleasures we experience. Still, we must also enjoy the moment and be comfortable, even in their absence.
- A sense of wealth comes from gradually developing unshakeable confidence to 'gain' in any environment.
- When we are comfortable with wealth and our personal ability to feel confident and effective, we are rewarded in both material and mental aspects.

---

29 Recall, the first is "Meet your Fate; Make your Destiny."

- An abundance mentality will lead to greater palpable abundance in many facets of life.

Another constraint resulting from the collective mnemonic's *virtual scorecard* is the worry arising from incorrect attitudes towards wealth. They can impact an individual and force feelings of inadequacy, causing unease, mental stress, and even schizoid reactions.

How can we become comfortable with wealth and how much we have? The effort we put in may only be one ingredient necessary to get a *sense* of wealth. Some put in enormous effort and still feel poor. Yet others acquire great wealth with what seems like little effort. Such contradictions plagued Nachiket because his attitude towards wealth, like several others, was mixed-up.

A burning desire for wealth causes confusion. There is a feeling of inadequacy with whatever wealth one already has and an incessant obsessive craving to possess more. So let me propose an alternative explanation of how we can be personally wealthy and confident, whether the quantum of wealth is in surplus or perceived deficit.

Despite the social temptations, which prompt us to treat wealth as a benchmark of success, you have it in you to enjoy the coffee and disregard the cup. This statement is based on a modern-day parable doing the rounds on the internet and goes as follows:

A group of alumni, well established in their careers, visited their old university professor. Conversation soon turned into complaints about stress in work and life. Then, the professor went to the kitchen and returned with a large pot of coffee and assorted cups. The cups were porcelain, plastic, glass, and crystal—some plain looking, some expensive, some exquisite. The professor asked that they help themselves to hot coffee.

When all the students had a cup of coffee in hand, the professor said, 'If you notice, all the nice-looking expensive cups were taken up first, leaving behind the plain and cheap ones. While it is normal for you to want only the best for yourselves: *that* is the source of your stress. All of you really wanted coffee, not the cup—but you consciously went for the best cups and were eyeing each other's cups.

If life is coffee, then the jobs, money, and positions in society are the cups. They are just tools to hold and contain life. But, sometimes, by concentrating only on the cup, people fail to enjoy its coffee.'

* * *

I'll begin with an attempt to annul any uneasiness about the distribution of wealth in society.

First, consider that longing for wealth could be a necessary lubricant for the civilization machine. We need some people to be dissatisfied with their wealth. The unhappy ones are occupied with increasing their wealth, which keeps the markets churning.

There must never be a satisfying amount or distribution of wealth in society if the capital markets and the value they generate are to sustain. Many would not risk investment without their yearning for more possessions and wealth. A person who flogs his horse of wealth due to dissatisfaction could be in a symbiotic relationship with those who find satisfaction in value creation.

Money needs to flow in society to avoid the ills of stagnation. Therefore, imbalances may be a natural way to keep it flowing. Just as we obtain electricity through the flow of water, the flow of money allows us to tap its power—the power of value. Imbalanced wealth could then be the engine for growth.

Wealth inspires value. On the flip side, value inspires wealth as well. We can desire wealth, but it is not advisable to be obsessed with measuring ourselves with wealth alone as a score. We cannot ignore or give lesser importance to value. Enjoy the value you create and rejoice in holistic betterment.

Nothing gets better in the real sense without an increase in value. In fact, even creating money *with* money is a recognized and valued profession. Therefore, we need a two-way relationship between players in the money game and other 'value' producers. Their relationship offers *valuable* outcomes.

* * *

There is yet another class of confusion relating to wealth. Consider the confusion arising from looking at wealth as an approval mechanism. Some historical standards endorse the mistaken notion that wealth will garner approval.

Again, this problem is created by popular yardsticks of success housed in the collective mnemonic. There is a lot out there to mislead us. Nachiket appears confused as well. He misinterpreted the purpose of wealth and saw it as a mechanism to garner approval. The kind of approval invited using wealth alone as a measure is usually sycophancy.

A conviction that approval is because of wealth comes from a lack of personal security and a lack of faith in oneself and Creation. There may never be a sense of achievement when self-esteem and personal success are measured against icons of wealth. There is always a Bill Gates, an Elon Musk, or a Jeff Bezos way ahead.

Even when in the right direction, all the steps we take will defy a sense of accomplishment using comparative and shifting yardsticks of wealth. The more a person tries for closure using only wealth as a measure, the more inadequate it will be. When one treats rewards differently, one sees wealth as a secondary benefit, not a primary goal.

The issue that makes people adopt comparative standards of wealth despite life meeting their needs is the constant parade of lifestyles deemed better. Ubiquitous media and marketing wizards are touting the great pleasures that wealth will confer upon us. However, pleasure is a one-way street.

Suppose we experience a higher form of pleasure. In that case, it is unlikely that the lesser ways will be adequate after that experience. If we reach beyond our capability for fun without a proper attitude, such experiences may tantalize and frustrate us.

Needless to add, there is always that fantastic holiday in the magnificent home of your schoolmate, the extravagant outing that your wealthy uncle sponsored; that lavish gourmet dinner your boss took you out to, or the texture of your neighbor's expensive designer dress brushing against you, or even that incredible electronic gizmo, which your kid played with at his friend's house, (about which *your* kid gets dreamy-eyed)... The serendipitous pleasures we may encounter are endless, restricted only by our imagination.

What kind of fate allows people to glimpse pleasure clearly outside today's menu, i.e., out-of-reach joys that we experienced, nonetheless? How can we cherish and not be downhearted about such experiences? Here, the individual must decide whether a form of pleasure is a personal goal.

Our goals for accomplishment and pleasure must follow more significant yet realistic personal needs. If it is practical and not fanciful, we can make such goals and desires part of our private purpose. It is a *need*.

We also should decide that having a need has nothing to do with enjoying today. Obsession destroys the moment. What is the difference between a person craving an abusive drug fix and desiring a form of acceptable pleasure? Nothing if one is uneasy without them. Don't destroy the moment by craving something way ahead in the future or something only remotely attainable, even when you have decided it's a *need*.

Would a shot of an expensive intoxicant enduringly solve problems? Will a custom-made perfume at $65,000 an ounce correct a self-esteem issue? Do you love your pet only because you decorate her with a diamond-studded *collar?* I think not. From today, let capability in the present, and the feasible capacities in the future, drive you to the pleasures of *your* life.

* * *

You have seen several people putting in more than a reasonable effort for personal wealth and glamour. Some harried executives, constantly traveling show-biz personalities, and the occasional ulcerated CEO would fit this description very well. Much of the mental and physical unease some are willing to go through for the sake of wealth is unimaginable.

The answer to why they do it could be fear of losing their lifestyle or parity and favor with *peers*. They are afraid to say, 'Enough.' They fear that enough may not be enough at some point. They are also among those who swing on the scales of comparative worth and cannot get off.

Nonetheless, we must appreciate that there are others who invest effort in acquiring or maintaining wealth because they have found more significant concerns. They do not focus just on personal wealth for motivation. They are the value-creators, and wealth to them is a consequence of being socially active.

Dr. Dharmaraj tried to make Nachiket see that chasing ever-increasing wealth would not increase security or satisfaction. We may need a shift in attitude to attain true comfort with our monetary goals and status. We can deliver value and excellence and get better holistically when our world does not revolve solely around wealth and its measurements.

The answer is to expand your goal to improve in multiple aspects, not just wealth. *The pursuit of happiness* is different from the pursuit of wealth. We would get better—and consequently, even wealthier—when we focus on creating value.

An abundance mentality leads to abundance. Expect that you will always have money, and you will have it. Uneasiness with cash leads to inappropriate drives and actions in managing wealth.

Imagine those who are uncomfortable with money. The minute such a person has more, he feels that things are abnormal. So, such people go and spend irrationally just to ease the discomfort or worry of having wealth. If we like to have money, money will stay with us.

The key to real wealth is to like it. Of course, this does not mean hoarding money but being comfortable with it. We should not find money sinful, wasteful, or unjust. When we become comfortable in our relationship with money, we discover wealth.

* * *

I hope the discussion helps manage any frustration with the distribution of wealth in society and any frustrating search to possess the greatest quantum of wealth we can have. While we can support the 'have-nots' with their needs, we need not compare the quantum of wealth with the 'haves.'

Wealth is not for approval. Wealth is not purely to make living pleasurable. Wealth comes through value, not the other way around. Beyond a certain threshold, *enough and more* are states of mind, not states of the material. Whatever you currently feel—as a have or a have not—you can get better and more successful if your personal outlook towards wealth is a sincere invitation.

The ultimate sense of security should come from your existence, learning, and betterment. Twists and turns in fate can bring or take away material wealth. However, if you groom yourself daily to do, learn, and enjoy in life... that is true wealth. Ask yourself—*Am I better equipped to deal with life today than a year ago?* For most of us, the answer is likely to be an emphatic 'YES!'

We *have* learned some lessons in the interim. When we prize growth and our ability to be proactive, whatever the circumstances, we come to appreciate the present and stay hopeful for the times to come.

Keep healthy growth, value, and learning as your measure of wealth. We will feel wealthy only when we discover this, whether we have no money, a few rupees, or millions in surplus.

* * *

In this Part III, we addressed the three problems pointed out in Part I and discussed how to build on the foundations set in Part II.

The next Part, Part IV, attempts to remove the chief doubts that restrict a positive and proactive mental outlook in the afflicted. It discusses ideas to lay to rest various inhibiting pressures in life. The objective is to enable us to drop off the questions: why conflict, why differences, why challenges, why be reasonable, and why traditional discord.

In Part IV are more explanations for several such 'whys' in our minds.

PART IV: The Confirmation

What's it all about? Why are we here? What's the point? Is there a point? Why bother? Why life?

At some point, you have probably pondered The Meaning of Life, and you came up with a satisfactory answer, which has, or has not, stood the test of time. Or you shrugged mightily, muttered, 'Beats the hell out of me,' and ordered another cheeseburger. *The Meaning of Life*. Very funny; very true.

The question that precedes 'What's the meaning of life?' is of course, '*Is there* a meaning to life?' Beats the hell out of me (again). I'm going to explore the first question as though the answer to the second question is yes.

If it's true that life has no meaning, no purpose, then it doesn't matter whether I've consumed a few pages speculating on it. So, let's play a game called Life Matters.

We'll start the game by *assuming* there is a purpose. The first question of Life Matters: What is the purpose of life? Here's my answer: Life is for doing, learning, and enjoying.

– Peter McWilliams (1949–2000), *Life 101* Series

CHAPTER 7

DIVERSITY

Nachiket took his chair, looking charged. 'Dr. Dharmaraj, I'm thinking more clearly, more often than before. I can direct my flow of thoughts and focus better. Does this mean I am forgetting the learning I thought I had from my past?' he asked.

'Nachiket, every mind is remarkable. The sooner you acknowledge that your thoughts are yours alone, the sooner you will be able to reap the benefits, past and present,' the doctor replied matter-of-factly.

'The more I write, the more convinced I am to be heard for what I am today. Not as some imaginary person from another life,' Nachiket said firmly.

'You have just begun to discover yourself as a unique individual. You can make personal choices now,' Dharmaraj said, barely hiding his delight at the progress Nachiket was making. 'It is, in a way, the awakening we discussed. You will find your chosen agreements and differences when you acknowledge that you can be in control.'

'But disagreement is conflict,' Nachiket observed. 'I had no doubts earlier, right or wrong! So, I wonder if that was more appropriate.'

'No, Nachiket. Your clarity has changed from a small to a large and more absolute perspective,' said Dharmaraj. 'The fear of standing up and disagreeing holds you back. Just imagine...if we all agreed on one side of the story, we would live in a lopsided world. So, it is important to disagree to maintain personal and political freedoms.'

'Are you saying there is no universal truth on which we can agree?' quizzed Nachiket.

The doctor spoke carefully. 'Assume there is such a thing momentarily but consider that the human mind is limited in its ability to understand it. Hence, in our limited fashion, we must choose a facet of the truth... while several facets may seem valid. We may or may not ever agree as a race,' said Dharmaraj, 'but unless we disagree, we will not go towards what may be a universal truth. So, we solve complexities, sort out disagreements, and get lifted to higher and higher planes of understanding.'

'Why should the Creator want this? That we should fight and disagree? Why not simply reveal the truth?' asked Nachiket.

'To paraphrase from a movie... Can you handle the truth?' said Dharmaraj with a pause. 'Imagine a limitless universe stretching way beyond our senses. Is it not good that our existence reveals it one moment at a time, one portion at a time, for us to fully experience? A limitless Universe we know exists, but we do not let it come in the way of our day-to-day life. Your existence will allow you to experience it a little at a time.'

'In other words,' Nachiket remarked, 'I was created with some limitations to experience the limitless from some standpoint.'

'An insightful observation... for if we were limitless, there would be no measurable experience!' exclaimed the doctor.

'But not everyone has the same limitations,' continued Nachiket. 'What to me is crystal clear may not be clear to someone else. This can cause conflict.'

'Yes,' the doctor agreed. 'To recognize mutual truths, we may undergo several iterations. However, it all becomes clearer with just the passing of time and keeping an open mind. If you still have conflict, then it is your chosen disagreement.'

'Then conflict is inevitable...?' posed Nachiket.

'Yes and no,' the doctor said, dragging the words out. 'You may have external conflict, but you do not have conflict within yourself once you think through your chosen disagreement. It could also be true that disagreements are how creation keeps its balance...'

'... or even provides the energy for its continued pulsing as it rocks back and forth?' said Nachiket, getting imaginative.

'Possibly,' conceded the doctor. 'It would be hard to get any movement or variety without attraction and repulsion. But this would not be the case in an existence where everything was uniform.'

'I begin to understand conflict when I take your words and add what I have learned from various scriptures,' said Nachiket pensively.

'And what is that?' asked the doctor.

'From the scriptures, we know there is a chosen duty, an altar for action despite any conflict. So, I think there is a personal answer in our lives,' reflected Nachiket.

'Nachiket, do take your medicines regularly. It will help you focus. Do you still hear voices?' inquired Dharmaraj.

'No... I feel I have brought my existence back within my body,' said Nachiket, smiling. 'The phantom sounds are just mumbles. I cannot make out what is being said. But then, I think if I was asked what the mumble is, I would decipher it as friendly.'

'Good! Good!' said the doctor. Clearly, the harmful symptoms were receding. What remained was to have Nachiket cope with the residual innocuous ones. 'Transcend any residual symptomatic triggers by either learning from them or by ignoring them. Here is a tip: Distract yourself by doing some light reading or listening to music. Have you been describing your history in your writings as I suggested?'

'Yes, I have, but there are some memories that won't leave me,' Nachiket confessed, stating a problem anybody could have. 'Some mistakes I have made haunt me.'

Real memories were now the basis for Nachiket's insecurities. Everyone has difficult memories. The likelihood of relapse was remote if Nachiket remained proactive.

'Let's explore how to manage these disturbing memories,' said the doctor, launching into another technique[30].

Nachiket needed to interact with others and realize that life did not challenge him alone—that life and its challenges were for everyone. He should understand that he could have a point of view, regardless of conflicting opinions. Moreover, he needed to realize that universal agreement or equilibrium is a perpetual work in progress.

DEFUSING DICTATORSHIP

Section Highlights

- Disagreements need to exist in society for checks and balances to be in place.
- When we do away with petty disagreements caused by envy, greed, wealth, power, and the like, core issues are what remain.
- Genuine differences keep cults, despots, and Orwellian nightmares away. They prevent monopolistic forces and isolating points of view from taking hold.
- There may be an in-built need for people to disagree so that better alternatives can emerge from such a churning.

One cannot exorcise the *disorienters* in the collective mnemonic completely. Many disorienting influences are deep-set. Some are obviously conflicting and compound the confusion experienced by a patient with schizophrenia.

---

30 See RI 3 "Forgive to Forget" at the end of the book under Recovery Instruments

There are many differences in practices and beliefs. Hence, doubts can crop up. One often harbors questions.

Why do several valid orientations or purposes exist? Why are there diverse rules and philosophies? Why so much difference in opinions on right and wrong? What justifies these different beliefs in creation and sometimes the need to fight for what we believe?

Questions like these triggered Nachiket's core unease and led to the larger disorder. Nachiket felt there should be no external conflict before choosing a purpose. The reason for this, again, could be the collective mnemonic. It has conflicting ideas but also houses a belief that there is some single universal truth with which all conflict can be overcome. Unfortunately, interpretations of social, religious, and political ideologies in the collective mnemonic mislead in their promise of a single Universal Law.

One suggestion is to leave the grandiose thoughts of an all-encompassing, all-pervading unity for now. It can distract one from understanding a personal purpose and the path to getting better. I claim that we need to recognize that different points of view are necessary for the effective functioning of humankind.

People need to disagree. When we experience conflict, this only moves disagreements to a higher plane. There is more significant learning on such a plane, and our choices become more evident. Let's check out three instances of conflict in our civilized society.

Conflict 1: Consider the continuing argument on whether businesses should be controlled by the government or just follow the principle of unbridled *laissez-faire*. Regardless of the growing global village, we cannot compromise the sovereignty of a country to accommodate corporate balance sheets. On the flip side, a nation is not sovereign because of its bureaucracy. Industry and State must be independent and act to balance the profit motive with fair practices. An industrialist cannot be an administrator of laws, and the State is not a business. Hopefully, these camps will always be distinct.

Conflict 2: What about the doctrines of vegetarianism and meat-eating? Arguing for vegetarians, the sourcing of meat is often brutal and painful. Arguing for meat-eaters, what one eats may not measure our compassion. Mother Teresa allegedly ate meat, and Hitler was a *flexitarian*[31]. Some research also claims vegetarians are more likely to have poor mental health from not ingesting meat with natural Omega-3 fatty acids. Then, there is the naïve question *Will our ecosystem remain balanced if the entire world turns vegetarian?*

Let's agree with any one side of this issue. It is essential to disagree to ensure continued balance. In this argument on being a vegetarian or a meat-eater, we can belong to one or the other camp; and continue the debate on it. The bottom line is that we were omnivores as a species, as evidenced by how our teeth have evolved. However, in the *present*, our choices may differ.

Conflict 3: Another continuing debate is between over-aggressive advertising and our right to privacy. An icon of advertising, Neil French, anonymously advertises a non-existent beer. Soon people are asking vehemently for the beer[32]. Then, he presumably, could sell the brand to a manufacturer *without a product in place*.

Early advertising objectively informed the public of the availability of a product or service. It did not overtly influence the buying decision. Advertising has changed dramatically since then. Nobel laureate in Literature Aleksandr Solzhenitsyn (1918-2008) was prompted by the proliferation of billboards to comment that it is a 'license to spit in the eye and soul of the passers-by.'

---

31 "Flexitarian" is a recent term coined to describe one whose diet is normally meatless but occasionally includes meat or fish. See http://www.merriam-webster.com/dictionary/flexitarian

32 This was done by him to collect data on the impact of *print* as a medium compared to other emergent media

Accepting the vital role advertising plays in keeping our news and entertainment within reach of our wallets, invasive advertising may still need regulation that ensures responsibility.

Dr. Dharmaraj was trying to clarify, through reasoning, as I attempted with the preceding simplistic examples, that personal purpose is not a one-point program. You could allow different points of view yet have a clear personal choice. When propaganda forces people to think alike, we may as well be heading towards a dictatorship or a terrorist group, or a cult.

How can we ensure conceptually brilliant but paranoid propaganda, such as that of extreme social order, does not enslave us? It seems critical that people think differently, *regardless of what appears right or wrong.*

* * *

The preceding arguments for opposing viewpoints may seem contrived, but they demonstrate why disagreeing is essential. Some issues should remain unresolved. The see-sawing conflicts are the bases of individual sovereignty. By opposing, people prevent the frightening scenario of powerful authoritarian control depicted in George Orwell's fiction.

Perhaps this is why the collective mnemonic is always a work-in-process. If it overwhelms us, our independence may be snatched. So, it must be perpetually flexible to take on fresh impressions as time marches on.

In a Hindu fable, a sparrow chased by a hawk takes refuge in the arms of Emperor Sibi. Emperor Sibi was known for his just decisions and compassion. To test him, the king of the lesser Gods, Indra, had taken the form of the sparrow, and Agni, the God of Fire, the hawk. The sparrow claimed protecting him was the emperor's duty. In contrast, the hawk claimed Sibi was denying him his natural prey and food. At this, Sibi offered an equal amount of his own flesh as food for the hawk as an alternative. The two gods then revealed themselves and showered their blessings on Sibi.

People play out a loftier personal purpose in their chosen agreements or disagreements. Many may face a nobler personal involvement at a tough crossroads, as did Sibi. However, when correctly directed, disputes rise to higher realms of relevance.

Of course, you are most welcome to disagree with such an idea. In fact, we all should agree to disagree for eternity. People should agree, nevertheless, within themselves. Such an integration carries us towards our chosen agreement or disagreement with a focus that translates into successful action.

* * *

Why do people disagree? People do choose differently and think differently. *Why does one person need persuading when another sees the same claim as a common truth? We have diverse backgrounds, but why doesn't the intellect's reasoning ability bring people together?*

We discussed why a universal truth is not ordained. We also examined why several points of view and versions need to exist. Now, can we argue that people are designed to disagree? For answers, let's look in the next section at that part of our physiology that houses our thinking, our brain.

DISAGREEMENT BY DESIGN

Section Highlights

- When any debate or conflict is genuine, reasonable, and humane, it contributes to us becoming more civilized as a race, regardless of the sides we choose.
- The roots of many conflicts may be in a flawed belief that there is a single goal that transcends all disagreement.

- Disagreement and conflict are inherent in our nature and may be evolutionary mechanisms for the human intellect.
- The trait of disagreement could be hardwired into the human brain's structure and a normal state for us as a species.

Scientists have reached some conclusions from split-brain research. In this, surgeons severed the connections between the left and right hemispheres of the brain for some patients whose medical conditions warranted such surgery.

When researchers showed an image of an object to the left-brain of these patients, the patients could name it. However, when they showed the same picture to the right-brain, the subjects could only pick out a similar object by feeling it. They could not name the thing, but they could sometimes articulate its use. It became clear that the left-brain is primarily responsible for symbolic communication (verbal) and the right-brain for understanding relationships in time and space (spatial).

It is unimportant whether the mapping based on the above pioneering study of the brain is accurate or not. At least one subsequent study indicates that the feminine left-brain can share spatial and verbal features[33]. What is more relevant is the brain's distinct verbal and spatial orientations. It means we have, at the minimum, two decision-making structures cooperating to make us whole.

Our brain's cognitive left portion typically attempts to understand using ordered patterns: lingual and other symbolic representations. At the same time, spatial arrangements are analyzed by the right half.

The collective mnemonic has been tutored over several ages by the human brain halves and vice versa. Some of the mnemonic's construction is a consequence of the left-brain being swayed by speculative right-

---

33 A study by Shaywitz, Bennet & Sally, reported in the New York Times, Feb 16th, 1995

brain inferences and the right brain being similarly affected by the left-brain. The results of this combination can sometimes be confusing to the witnessing self.

Additionally, researchers' brain mapping links the hind-brain to the senses and the fore-brain to motion. Adding more complexity is that the right half of the brain controls the motor actions of the left side of the body and vice versa.

Are these factors relating to the design and functioning of the brain causing confusion in us? Is this why we do not agree as a race?

I argue that our brain sometimes delivers mixed signals because it uses diverse physiological locations and numerous crisscrossing neural networks. Random thoughts crop up during discussions of important issues, leading decisions astray. A misplaced emotion or an awkward gesture intrudes into the smooth flow of a conversation. Sometimes, we blank out at an unsuitable moment while trying to analyze an issue.

A case in point, *deja-vu* is hypothesized to occur because of reversed timing in the receiving of stimulus by different parts of the brain. That is, stimuli are received by the *memory location* in the brain, a fraction before the *conscious portion*. This leads to the person feeling he has already experienced what is perceived.

The brain's design of differing locations for action and reaction means that thinking can take many directions within the brain's structure at any time. As a result, the brain can reach vast and potentially bewildering arrays of conclusions as a thinking tool. So, it is no surprise that different people use this tool to reach differing conclusions.

These aspects of the brain could interrupt one person's understanding of another during any interaction. The brain's functioning can be confusing, and its design innately causes disagreements.

* * *

Some patients with schizophrenia may vehemently look for an all-encompassing, zero-conflict state to find answers to their confusion. Unfortunately, such a state is not possible. Although popular thought proclaims that there is a single universal truth or destination for people to achieve, disagreement may really be the normal state.

Beliefs have been carried over from when races were geographically distributed, speaking different languages and practicing different customs. Therefore, ideological stubbornness continues in many. However, with fresh understanding, isolating propaganda, poetry, or passion that makes for warring factions will not sweep us off our feet.

Has some force, divine or mundane, designed us to disagree so that we can discover what our personal disagreement should be?

Who knows? Perhaps our physiological design makes human disagreement and perpetual conflict normal. Though people find it unpleasant, the social purpose of debate is clear, as suggested by the sampling of opposites in the previous section, *Defusing Dictatorship*.

Does the grand design demand that our ideas differ perpetually?

We can agree or disagree according to our personal choice and yet look objectively at other alternatives. We can admit different constructive beliefs or understanding, though we do not agree with some (or all) of their tenets. We can disagree and yet, live and let live. How do we do this? We must understand 'reasonableness.'

CHAPTER 8

REASONABLENESS

Over the next sessions, Dr. Dharmaraj attempted to convert any of Nachiket's remaining indignation and despair over his perceived handicap into motivation.

'We cannot always choose what life hands out to us. The positive thing from the experience is that you can now take a good, objective look at yourself. As I said before, this is more than what some normal people get to do in their entire lives. Most of us float along, going where the tides take us. But no! You sense your current circumstance and perceive a need to do something. This is actually good, Nachiket.'

'My mind is filled with ideas to take shortcuts. I want to be on a social par with those my age, and I am willing to do anything...even bend the rules, if necessary!' exclaimed Nachiket.

Dharmaraj asked, 'What do you have in mind?'

'The thought of buying a fake college degree to ease getting employed has crossed my mind,' Nachiket answered.

'Nachiket, you can get a genuine degree with effort if you choose to. We all have extraordinary minds and just need the lubrication of effort. Practice getting good at something. So many vocations have innovation and creativity outside of academics,' the doctor said.

'Much useless information is driven into us in the name of a college education. They don't teach the important things, such as developing emotional maturity, the ability to read people, or other skills that help in social interaction. They are only playing with semantics.' Nachiket felt that academics had not prepared him to meet the practical.

'As a discerning human being, you know the difference between nonsense and sense, even if it's only from your perspective,' the doctor ventured. 'You must grant there could be others who see your idea of sense as nonsensical too. I agree that education may seem to be an exercise in semantics until it is applied.

Any knowledge and skill we cannot apply is trivia. In fact, a CEO, when asked what he would pay a top-notch quizzer, replied, "About the cost of a decent encyclopedia." Applying any knowledge we gain makes us see sense in it. But to be able to use it, you first must make the effort of learning.'

'Yes, that could be true,' conceded Nachiket.

'If you see that as possible, you can see any value-adding knowledge or skill as reasonable,' the doctor said. 'You may disagree with, but not deny, other forms of understanding.'

'The problem is when others' understanding and achievements clash with mine. For instance, they could do things to undermine me,' said Nachiket. 'They may mock me about being slow...'

'You must choose your convictions now after due diligence. Be strong and disagree where you must... Being reasonable does not mean turning the other cheek all the time. If you firmly anchor your beliefs in getting better, no one will affect you at the core.

If you feel taunted, step back from the situation and rehearse progressive and confident thoughts. Then, the similar issues you encounter going forward do not affect you as much. When you are not reacting with misdirected emotions, you can correctly and proactively apply your knowledge and experience,' advised the doctor.

'I have had this experience and lost time,' said Nachiket, still hesitant. 'It seems cruel to hide so much from me and then reveal it only when I have lost time.'

'The truth, Nachiket, can be hard. However, do you realize you are one of the few who can see it as an actionable truth? What if I told you there are several with similar experiences who remain deluded or desperate? Life has given you a chance to start anew. Denial of your birthright to choose is worse than any delay.'

'I have lost so much time...can I live a life that is true now?' asked a genuinely concerned Nachiket. 'Will my life ever be without limitations?'

'Wisdom changes a person.' Dharmaraj said. 'We can only dream of going back to a carefree childhood. We must take the responsibility to move ahead in time as adults while nurturing what is left of the child within us.

The time you have lost is insignificant compared with the time you can lose by being aware and still doing nothing. Appreciate the smallest of your achievements and gradually challenge yourself to do bigger things. Don't feel limited; choose your own reasonable and appealing concerns.'

'How can I start on a clean slate when so much has already happened?' pondered Nachiket, pressing the point.

'Assume that all you experienced and your position in life today were pre-determined...that all you are is the result of choices you made without knowing. You are now in control of your choices *from this point forward*. OWN your life NOW, Nachiket! A chance to live anew is yours. Now, you can do with it as you wish.'

'I feel like the prisoner who, after many years in captivity, wanted to return to his cell when he was freed,' said Nachiket, still sorry for himself.

'You have the knowledge and the capability now,' the doctor said. 'Look forward, look outward…make small but sure steps, and soon you will make huge strides. Your willingness to do this will create a firm intent. Your intent will create your motivation, and your motivation will give you success. So first, just be willing. The rest will follow.'

The doctor realized Nachiket could take a little more time to deal with his condition, even though medicine was controlling the positive symptoms of schizophrenia. Because of the treatment, he had no disturbing hallucinations, and his delusions had receded. However, for Nachiket to return to the mainstream, he would also need to overcome the negative symptoms of schizophrenia (such as social withdrawal, lack of motivation, and the like).

Dr. Dharmaraj knew that there was a danger of depression with growing insight. Pressing questions such as *Why me?* Or anxiety about the enormous challenge that was just beginning could cause feelings of darkness.

So, the doctor decided to wait for a sure sign before resorting to the general counseling he had in mind for Nachiket. His patient first had to move from denial to acceptance and become capable of proactively bettering his situation.

RIGHTS AND REASONS

Section Highlights

- We can never get started on the path of practical personal purpose unless we 'unask' the question: What causes us to exist?
- Being unreasonable could seem the right way to act for some as they see the forces behind creation as malevolent and life as a free-for-all with no rules.

- There are some common, inherent, and reasonable rules or rights that everyone desires, allowing us to conclude that being reasonable is an available choice for us.
- Since such rights are desired by all people, both reasonable and unreasonable, we can use them as touchstones to evaluate the validity of our actions.
- With the correct information, being reasonable can become a state of mind and a powerful survival strategy for us.

Let me try and dispense with the questions that Nachiket had, many of which are common when the afflicted are gaining insight. *Why get started? Why should I seek betterment? Why do I need to put in any effort when I feel fate has dealt me a bad set of cards? Why be responsible? Why be reasonable when I do not see reasonableness in my life?*

While we know what a good attitude should be, we could be hesitant or skeptical. For example, one could ask, *I think I know what I must do, but what about how things are?* This is because life can pit us against capable people and make us face novel challenges. Therefore, some may doubt whether having a personal purpose in this *competitive* age is feasible.

Perhaps our 'competition' has been aware for much longer, making them more prepared. One could debunk life, tuck in, ask why, and want the scoreboard reset. Alternatively, many think of shortcuts, as Nachiket contemplated.

Life is not fair in the conventional sense. Therefore, coming to terms with reality might be more important than finding answers for every injustice. Why be reasonable, righteous, and resolute, despite a perceived host of reasons not to be so?

There just *could be* reasons to be sensible that are very practical. It could be time to try a new outlook, not merely ask '*Why?*'

* * *

The reason for the universe's Grand Design, with or without other literate or intelligent life, is unknown. Whether there is a rudimentary life-form anywhere else or any God-like caretaker(s) for this Grand Design is unproven. We could choose to thank or pray to, apologize to, curse, and swear at... even ignore Him, Her, It, or Them (whatever is responsible for us being alive). Nevertheless, creation *IS*, whether its cause is divine or mundane because we *ARE* here now.

A primary question, *'Who is the reason?'* might only have answers in theology. The secondary query, *'Why should I be reasonable?'* draws license from the lack of a clear answer to the primary question. This query is at the core of a fundamentally misplaced rebellious spirit. Such a spirit feels there is no cause to be reasonable (or civil) if no one or nothing is in charge.

If no one is responsible for the creation we know, the rebel in us may conclude: What I think, say, or do, cannot matter.

We need to 'unask' the question, *'Who or what is the reason?'* This leads to accepting our being here now, instead of a frustrating search to become something else, fashioned synthetically by social or religious standards. If the utility of positive living becomes evident, we can 'unask' the question.

Nachiket discusses religion a little later in the book. Here, I try a logical approach to support reasonable living instead of doing it just because of religious or social compulsions.

This chapter argues that being *good* works as a survival strategy; we need not be reasonable merely because theology, religion, or social diktats demand that we be so.

* * *

Most of us can recognize what is responsible and what is not. The most unreasonable person on the face of the Earth, if sane, can identify reasonable behavior. Now note that irresponsibility only occurs if transgressions or disrespect of some rights or duties happen. Since, as intelligent humans, we realize responsible and irresponsible behavior, it follows that there probably *are* rights common to all individuals.

As examples of our rights, some quite simply are:

- The right to valid information.
- The right to agree or disagree with proposed exchanges and transactions.
- The right to fair benefit in exchanging material, emotional and intellectual value.

To elaborate on these examples, when a person uses the tools of propaganda to disseminate incorrect information, they transgress the first right. When a person forces the exchange of goods and services without knowledge and agreement, the person violates the second right. Finally, the third right is transgressed when we cannot benefit mentally or materially from the value we have to offer.

We can best understand the responsibility to be reasonable when we appreciate such inherent rights and use them as touchstones to evaluate behavior.

Consider that those who are unreasonable, despite their wrongdoings, would also desire such rights in their favor. Everyone is likely to want these, regardless of their faith, social stature, or on whichever side of the moral divide they feel they belong. Hence, they are Universal. Let us hazard that the rights like those proposed define civilized behavior and can be offered in defense of being personally reasonable.

Several convincing reasons and pressures to be unreasonable and transgress these rights exist. For instance, ironically, believing in a benevolent and forgiving universe or force may lead to perverseness, as such a force would not punish people. It is a logical somersault from the argument that if the universal creative force were malevolent or maleficent, what we do may be inconsequential.

Constant change is another reason for being unreasonable. When the rules change constantly, people see no reason to be reasonable. For example, I have a job today; tomorrow, the company might lay me off due to downsizing or fraud. The Hollywood comedy, *Fun with Dick and Jane* parodied this. The couple in the movie takes to robbery to maintain their lifestyle after the CEO embezzles the company providing their livelihood.

Further reasons to support being unreasonable are from beliefs that the imbalances in our world cannot be resolved. For example, there will be rich and developing countries with more affluent or impoverished people. Many people find reasons to be unreasonable because of such social conditions. They perceive injustice in the world and hence rationalize being unreasonable.

This class misses out on the benefit of looking at themselves supportively and compassionately, convinced that consistent reasonableness is unnatural.

The power to distinguish between reasonable and unreasonable behavior is already in us. Whether a person chooses to act unreasonably (transgressing the rights of others) or reasonably (respecting the rights of others) depends on the pull of a personally realized greater good over any destructive bias.

In the following three sections, I attempt to challenge reasons to be unreasonable from new directions.

THE SYNTHETIC SUSPICION

Section Highlights

- As an elementary argument for reasonableness, we humans do have the ability to recognize (un) reasonable behavior.
- Some feel that reasonableness is idealistic, unnatural, and synthetic because much of our reasoning is in language, and language is absent in raw Nature.

- Several ugly truths in creation could also force some to consider being unreasonable.
- We should see unfortunate or unreasonable truths as inferior to progressive and constructive happenings.
- Reasonableness is a key that can unlock a powerful sense of purpose. It can open the way for living with a sense of belonging, transcending comparisons or doubt.

Let's explore why many afflicted and even supposedly ordinary people are inclined to act unreasonably.

Firstly, a person may choose to be unreasonable because he feels the whole edifice of human knowledge and understanding is an elaborate lie. Some may think that the available information does not explain reality, so the entire theoretical edifice is false.

One could also feel that knowledge is an ever-shifting collection with no permanence and find this an acceptable excuse to be unreasonable.

For example, a widespread belief held for a long time was that the earth is flat. Scientific revelations discarded this *knowledge*. Since there cannot be absolute, unchanging knowledge, one could argue why to bother with being reasonable.

Is the human repository of information cheating us? Is the environment subjecting people to a huge knowledge hoax?

But of course, if all knowledge were a hoax, what you are reading now would not make sense. If all recorded human knowledge were an elaborate lie, any learning we come across would be false. But this is not so. Some knowledge endures the test of time.

How is knowledge credible? In its representation by language (words or symbols), the formation of objective meaning is something we take for granted. Since you can read this and accept or reject it, literacy has meaning for you. People choose what truth is and what a lie is in the spoken and written word.

We reflect on fact and fiction so we can choose to make some ideas our own and disregard the rest. Most of us possess the faculty to distinguish between reasonable and unreasonable. We can appreciate our capacity to select and choose information to internalize. Therefore, we cannot discard all understanding as an outrageous lie.

Conclusion #1: Life has in it, at the very least, the scope for deriving reason and reasonableness.

To the literate, language, including the written word is not voodoo but a *fait accompli*. It is an extraordinary miracle we take for granted. We already know Nature has an illiterate side, as explored in Part 1. Nachiket felt that recorded knowledge is synthetic because language does not seem intuitive or natural. *Language, especially in its written form, is unnatural.*

This is the second reason people doubt recorded sense and knowledge. If one finds it hard to trust theoretical communication, it could be because of nature's illiteracy.

Conclusion #2: The reasonable side of recorded human knowledge may seem abnormal because our natural roots are illiterate.

Strangely, the truth can also cause a person to be unreasonable. This is our third reason why being unreasonable may seem appropriate to some.

In the classic *Gone with the Wind*, Scarlett O'Hara has her decisive moment when she is hungry and impoverished. She swears, 'God as my witness, I will get through this if I must lie and cheat... [And when I get over this] I will never go hungry again.' A bitter truth may force a person to be unreasonable.

Actually, any compromise stemming from the methods of truth could be more inappropriate than a compassionate lie. The ways of truth conjure what appears to be fact. These methods commonly determine what is eventually accepted and what is rejected, regardless of reality. A couple of examples, both a tad contrived, could clarify this.

A man declares a hunger-strike for a political cause. He fasts until he is at death's door. He then tries to communicate in a fragile state. His garbled statement seems decipherable as a desire to end the fast. His overzealous followers deny him any compromise and delay medical support.

The man dies fasting. His followers tell the media he died in his hunger-strike for the cause. This is the truth. They also say to the press that medical support was attempted. This is also the truth. This, then, is the harm of using the truth methods alone.

Fact, sometimes, is typically deduced rather than evident. People could therefore manipulate the methods of truth. In this case, a type of truth concealed a weak fasting man's need. It could well be that the man realized the enormous repercussions of carrying out his martyrdom and wanted to suggest something constructive. But unfortunately, what would have resulted instead are probably riots, infighting, and social unrest.

A conjured truth might become established and lead to chaos. It is not false, but it could be a manipulated and 'wrong' truth (a deceptive truth).

Now consider a man with very weak eyesight (again) at death's door. He asks to see his daughter, and the relatives summon her. By the time she arrives, he is gone. He, however, dies believing he has seen his daughter because a niece impersonated his daughter when all hope that she would make it on time was lost. He died smiling peacefully, thinking it was his daughter he saw in his last few moments.

Truths arising from deductions alone, or those with no verifiable substance behind them, could cause more harm than help, as in the example of the fasting man. But, further, we can resolve or mitigate bitter or ugly truths best by a progressive nudge, as in the case of the dying man with weak eyesight.

We possess the faculty to choose between an unreasonable truth and a reasonable lie. A lie that helps and is considerate would usually be harmless. But, on the other hand, the truth sometimes hurts.

For example, we refrain from commenting on a person's looks or afflictions. Body-shaming and mental health stigma are deplorable. Instead, compassion and sensitivity are called for.

I hazard that for us to shun being unreasonable, we need to shift reliance from what appears to be the truth to what is constructive or compassionate. We need not succumb to unwarranted truths and move our beliefs to that which is progressive instead. This outlook can inspire a good attitude over the unreasonable.

Conclusion #3: We need to invalidate the ugly, sometimes manipulated, truths we experience in favor of progressive happenings.

* * *

Can we be anything other than reasonable towards ourselves as an argument favoring reasonableness? Then reasonableness must be natural, right?

Unexplainable fate, or the acts of unreasonable people, may have brought you to where you are. However, when you take that as a given, as something you must accept, you can act and no longer just react. Suddenly, there is utility instead of futility in everything. Any vexations to the spirit become manageable.

You begin to feel that the very question, *Why life?* is unnatural and a synthetic suspicion. Instead, you experience living as unique—your birth, existing, and journey forward, flaws and all. We can accept and move.

Now, consider the categorical disclaimer next: I did not choose to be born and be a human being. Does this give us the right to be unreasonable? This is the ultimate reluctance to own life. It deserves an entire section.

THE NASCENT NOTION

Section Highlights

- People who question life instead of accepting and acting in it are unreasonable and destructive.
- There is a personal choice in being born, even when rationalized and reduced to a minuscule one.
- Accepting this nascent choice could mean the difference between owning and enjoying life or being reckless and irresponsible.
- Successful living also depends on owning one's life and having faith in its abundance in some manner or another.

In a strange case, an infertile couple asked a woman to be a surrogate mother to a baby from the sperm of a donor selected by them. This led to a legal tangle after the couple broke up. Courts had to conform to laws and precedents and could not determine who was responsible for the nurture of the child.

They could not pin the responsibility on the infertile 'father' or 'mother,' the surrogate mother, or the anonymous donor[34]. Our society brought an orphan into existence.

How do we explain such a birth? It is just one of those puzzles for humankind to ponder. But unfortunately, seeing puzzles of this kind may cause afflicted individuals to question the reason for their existence and to shift responsibility or the blame.

---

34 Reported on 2 February 1998 in The Hindu a national Indian newspaper, based on a US news agency report.

If we feel our predecessors made the decision for us to exist, look at the natural choice we all made. We all emerged from the union of an egg and an incredibly determined sperm, beating the odds of many millions to one.

Looking at an exception provided by science to conceiving naturally only makes the choice more profound. This exception is a procedure called Intra Cytoplasmic Sperm Injection (ICSI - Icksee).

Doctors pick up and inject sperm into an egg using a special pipette. This pipette sucks in the genetic coding in the sperm. The code is then pierced into the egg and released. ICSI, done first in 1992, claims successful impregnation in cases with extremely low sperm counts and virtually no motility (the ability of sperm to swim).

We can argue that a sperm cell in such a procedure exercises no choice. However, consider that there is a drive to exist regardless of the method of fertilization. Even if we were test-tube babies, we would still exhibit a natural choice to live.

The embryo's intrinsic tendency to develop is an expression of an automatic intention to come alive. Once activated, the *need* for the package of genetic information to develop into a baby seems inherent. In other words, no fertilized egg self-destructs.

Whatever the odds, there is a drive to exist regardless of the being's chances to perform well in its environment. An example is the Rhesus factor conflict, where a fertilized egg still 'wants' to exist despite the intolerance of the birthing environment[35]. Therefore, we might be able to consider that a more profound choice to live is inherent in the sperm and egg. This package exercises the option to be born.

At first reckoning, the choice of an embryonic cell to develop seems no different from lower life-forms or some mindless force. The distinction

---

35 The Rh disease occurs when there is an incompatibility between the blood types of the mother and the fetus

is in recognizing that this single cell has the blueprint of a thinking feeling and complex life-form, with the potential to contemplate the mysteries of the universe.

In regression to its beginnings, our mind existed in a nascent form. It knew no words or meaning, but it had enough individual drive to play out its creation. It chose to live when it had the chance to do so.

This raises the question: *Why should a person with a challenging disability be born? Why would parents choose to bring a child with a congenital disability into the world when it could invite cruelty?* This is where we must acknowledge the mission over the mistake. We must view the blemishes and conflicts in Creation as puzzles or missions for humankind.

Just as the example of the orphan child we began this section with, such births could be problems for us to resolve in the long run. They are questions posed by time for human development to answer. They are missions that beg humanity to realize that we must yet cooperate as a race despite different points of view. Although it inevitably invites some debate, we can recognize these are not *divine* mistakes (See the text: *"Design, Default or Deviation"*).

Denying any stake in our own creation, flaws and all, denies our power to heal, learn, and enjoy.

Conclusion #4: Being born has an element of choice, however minuscule. Accepting this possibility would help us differentiate unreasonableness from mature responsibility.

The four conclusions outlined are meant to reassure us that we can be reasonable and succeed. We need not see our situation as one that demands devious effort, whether we are ordinary or afflicted. I emphasize that this is a prerequisite for donning life's obligations or missions reasonably; we need to own life, flaws and all, to progress.

* * *

Design, Default, or Deviation

A related and controversial issue is the continuing debate on abortion between pro-life and pro-choice groups[36]. There could be many reasons for opting to terminate a mistake of irresponsible coitus. Amongst these is that the life-form cannot be cared for in the circumstances. Could this primal being have been born to live a full life without harming itself or its circle of humanity? Can humanity be the judge of that? The Bible says, 'Thou shalt not kill;' it, prima facie, begs the argument, 'Thou shalt allow birth;' or, does it?

John Donohue (Stanford Law School) & Steven Levitt (The University of Chicago) reached some novel conclusions in their paper 'The Impact of Legalized Abortion on Crime' in The Quarterly Journal of Economics *dated May 2001. They attributed as much as half the sharp drop in American crime rates in the 1990s to the 1973 Roe vs. Wade decision by the Supreme Court, legalizing abortion throughout the USA. When linked to peak criminal activity in the age of 18-24, the sequential drop in crime rates in each State follows their sequential adoption of legalized abortion. The research suggests that the abortion of a fetus with lesser chances for social success could preempt criminal activity later in life.*

There is inexcusable ignorance or deliberate stupidity at the root of this debate because modern science provides us with enough options to prevent such dilemmas. Therefore, we can take preventive action. We can reject rigid beliefs or religious orthodoxy and favor social stability for the agents, their progeny, and our community. In that case, we will see a 'greater good' in taking prophylactic steps.

Given our empowerment by law, we have the right to take either decision. Any decision within a period pre-empting discernible human features, such as the sex of the embryo, does seem faultless. When we can take the responsibility to create a primal being, we may then be able to take responsibility for terminating it before it becomes manifest as well.

---

36 Another reason to add to why we need to disagree as a species.

Still, there are no conclusive arguments favoring one side over the other. So, we must choose without fear of human or divine retribution as the basis for our choice.

* * *

Life can be reasonable and rewarding in some aspect or the other. Successful living depends on owning one's life as unique and having faith in its abundance. We can realize the richness of personal reason (and reasonableness) when we remain open to receiving this in one manner or another.

JUDO JUDGMENTS

Section Highlights

- Popular standards tend to promote aggression and confrontation as traits that display confidence.
- Many downplay the role of peaceable reasonableness as a successful survival strategy.
- However, some scientific research indicates that reasonableness and selective cooperation are the best survival strategies.
- The only unfairness that seems 'acceptable' is when we respond in the same vein after offering cooperation a couple of times—a strategy called cooperative reciprocity.

Irrespective of affliction or a sense of inadequacy, a body of research suggests a sound rationale to be reasonable in our dealings. Though some aspects of our existential deck seem stacked against being good and sensible, the success of unreasonableness appears short-lived.

No enduring theoretical or practical justification exists for worldviews promoting corrupt or unreasonable action.

Therefore, being reasonable is not merely for us to conform to social or religious correctness. Instead, it is because the success of other survival strategies seems susceptible to friction, psychosocial conflict, and other personal and social breakdowns. An unrelenting aggressive stance in our dealings may eventually lead to collective self-destruction.

* * *

Consider this information about John Maynard Smith's (1920–2004) findings from the book *One Percent Advantage*. A pre-eminent academician,[37] he was responsible for pioneering work on *evolutionarily stable strategy*. He mathematically proved that the average outcome is a decline in societies where aggressive encounters are more than a rarity. However, a mixed culture comprising aggressive and passive individuals would result in stability.

The growth and proportion of aggressive and passive individuals in a diverse society remain stable. This is probably because tolerant individuals survive encounters through defensive strategies. The aggressive individuals, in contrast, injure their own kind due to infighting. For comparison, the researchers used communities of hawks and doves in their studies.

In addition to inferences from the preceding, we can draw some allied conclusions from Robert Axelrod's[38] and William D Hamilton's[39] (1935–2000) work. This work involved setting up survival strategies that faced off in a computer game (like chess programs). In the experiment, they built different behavioral models: players who did the opposite of the opponent and some acting randomly. Finally, after running several game variations, a preferred strategy that led to victory turned up. They called it Tit-for-Tat.

---

37 Gribben, John and Mary. *The One Percent Advantage*. Boston: Twayne Publishers, 1988
38 Robert Axelrod is an American political scientist from the University of Michigan
39 William Hamilton was a significant British evolutionary theorists of the 20th century

It had only two rules: On the first move, cooperate; afterward, respond by doing what your opponent did. The second round of computer simulation involved sixty-two entries designed to meet the challenge of beating the Tit-for-Tat strategy. The simulation iterated over three million choices. This came up with the same result.

Tit-for-Tat was further refined to *forgive* one more unfriendly act. It ignored an opponent's unfriendly act for a second time, offering cooperation once more before copying the other player's approach. This refinement made the strategy work even more successfully.

It is an 'evolutionarily stable strategy' with a vengeance. The strategy works as an effective tool in interactions. It is also a reasonable choice. Like Judo, it uses the opponent's own moves against him.

Tit-for-Tat is a 'strategy of cooperation based on reciprocity.' according to Robert Trivers. Dr. Trivers is one of the most influential evolutionary theorists of this age.[40]

Purposeful living would then be a series of reasonable choices that develop progressive *karma*. Though the response may seem uncivil, responding in the same measure is the only proviso that could be an acceptable compromise of the reasonable.

Dharmaraj made it clear in his dialogues that he was not asking Nachiket to always turn the other cheek. So, we will see how to practically apply 'cooperative reciprocity' later in the book.

* * *

The two chief ideas in the preceding sections are that there are reasons to be reasonable and there should be a willingness to own life.

---

40 Dr Robert Trivers was originally Professor of Anthropology and Biological Sciences at Rutgers University, USA. He is now President, Biosocial Research Foundation, Millstone, NJ

Fundamental reasonableness requires a shift in perspective, realizing that you can accept your circumstances and change them if needed. Then, finally, you get to a point where you can declare you are not a victim, whether afflicted or ordinary.

Some of life's challenges may seem unreasonable and unjust. However, if we *accept and act* on life's personal, professional, and social presentations, we can feel motivated, even if the challenges are demanding.

What if changing our situation seems impossible, even when willing to try? What is our takeaway when our circumstances take an interminably long time to change... if they change? How can we attempt to be reasonable when our challenges seem impossible to get over? A brief discussion on 'Challenge' is in our next chapter.

CHAPTER 9

CHALLENGE

'I have to keep this meeting short,' said Dr. Dharmaraj. 'I understand you wanted to meet me urgently....' The doctor was beginning to worry that Nachiket was growing dependent on him and wanted to wean him away as he showed improvement.

'I have just a few quick questions,' responded Nachiket. 'I am still unsure why I have this condition's challenge. Challenge is ubiquitous—in youth and in old age.'

'More reason to see that it has a purpose,' explained the doctor. 'Every challenge, big and small, have hidden lessons; a special learning for you when you do not buckle under it.'

'Why should life be so? Going from challenge to challenge? Isn't there an easier way to teach?' inquired Nachiket.

'What if I told you that there was some knowledge meant for you that no one else would get? The learning is very exclusive and personal. Life gives lessons to each according to one's own need.'

'Is there a point where challenges end?' asked Nachiket.

'When challenges end, the guiding force in us no longer exists.' Dharmaraj said with finality. 'Challenge provides us with choices of directions to take and destinations to seek. When we move towards these destinations, the benefits become obvious.'

'My purpose seems to be in the challenge I choose...' said Nachiket, beginning to understand.

'... Or in the challenges bestowed on you,' completed the doctor. 'For example, consider that your condition has given you a unique opportunity to view life differently.'

'I know some things several others don't....' said a clued-up Nachiket.

'Exactly!' said the doctor.

'I suddenly feel lonely, and the prospect of an entire life looming ahead of me... fighting challenges... growing old...' switched Nachiket, a little despondently.

'Every day is an opportunity to learn,' the doctor responded. 'You have had this experience. Already you are learning from it, and I have no doubt you will do well. You see obstacles where I see opportunities.'

'But we do get older...' said Nachiket, thinking of the challenges of old age. 'What is the opportunity when instead of getting better, we get worse?'

'Change the perspective,' the doctor replied. 'The fact is, although we seem worse off in some respects as we get older, we can get better in others. So, you must focus on what you can do and the learning you inevitably obtain.'

'Does this mean my getting better will extend into old age?' Nachiket asked.

The doctor clarified. 'The yardsticks by which you measure betterment need to change. Today you may focus on physical and material goals. Later in life, emotional and spiritual goals may become as important. It is only a change in perspective to the basic direction of improving continuously. Think about it.'

The doctor did not tinker with his prescription. Nachiket only had real doubts about existence. This was a clear sign that he was out of his delusional world. His fears about getting old were no different from those of others. The doctor allayed Nachiket's fears with explanations and suggested some reading[41].

Dharmaraj advised the parents to keep up the medication and take Nachiket to informal social gatherings or places where he would not feel threatened.

THE HIDDEN NAVIGATOR

Section Highlights

- Being reasonable is difficult when faced with challenges that appear insurmountable.
- But, without challenges, big and small, there is only uniform aimlessness or a state where our competencies remain dormant.
- There is learning and direction when we adopt and respect challenges as part of our existential purpose.
- As we get older, challenges change. So, we should adapt and choose new ones.

Is life an accident in the cosmos? Is the intellect a deviation from the norms of Nature? Should people just stop questioning and exist, as Sartre suggested? Does living have a point? Does it need to have a point?

Several of us have considered these questions sometime in our lives. Yet, many dismiss such queries and get on with our affairs, preparing breakfast, passing the sauce, and paying the bills.

While such questions seem passé given the exhilarating pace of this age, they acquire significance because this quicker pace brings novel challenges. When an afflicted individual confronts such challenges, he could question why they are even there.

---

41 See RI 4 *"Find Gold in Old"* at the end of the book under Recovery Instruments

Adverse changes in our circumstances could create perceptions of unreasonable challenges. In some challenging settings, a person may feel ill-equipped. Yet other events test a person's comfort zone severely. While this can occur for any individual, it is common for someone with a mental affliction.

Due to his bizarre experiences, Nachiket saw never-ending challenges instead of opportunities. He was treading water instead of swimming. Like several out there, he asked, '*Why this challenge? Why do I lack clear abilities when others are well-equipped? Why do others find it necessary to challenge me? Why do challenges keep disturbing the comfort I have with myself? Why is life challenging?*' Let's see how we can view challenges positively.

* * *

As an explanation for challenges, I first go on the beaten track. The 'bad' and challenging life elements may be a deliberate design flaw. This means that just as the bigger trials and tribulations are missions for humankind, the more bite-sized ones may be for us to resolve as individuals. This is the Creator's, or Nature's, way of getting us ready for the long haul.

Readiness is the mental state to face our unique reality. For example, a surgeon should practice being ready and not get sick at the sight of blood. Small challenges could be like the prick and intent of a vaccine, which develops our ability to meet more enormous, similar challenges.

Our readiness to accept small challenges is the preparation to take on more significant problems. The key is to recognize that we are consistently better equipped to face challenges and to treat *that* as *manna*. We reject the gifts, sometimes subtle and intangible, that problems and difficulties bring when we do not meet them head-on.

* * *

The Japanese, in the past, used to have the concept of lifetime employment. How did it work? How do you get people to work productively without threatening them with losing their income or livelihood?

When asked how they oversaw the shirkers, one manager replied, 'We give them a chair, a desk, and possibly a window. Not a single shred of work goes their way. They are not socially isolated but made to feel that time hangs heavy. In most cases, they started looking for things to do after a while or left to do something independently.'

As the preceding suggests, people can degenerate and decay or improve and flourish from a null state. Challenge is the appearance of a middle ground that provides a recogniz*able choice of direction* in life. The problems we grasp as our own offer us a sense of purpose.

Take away the 'bad' and the challenging, and people would be directionless. We could go the distance without going anywhere. No beginning, no end, and nothing in between. What would exist is a uniform aimlessness or a competent but still dormant state. Introduce challenges, and *presto*—we have direction.

Now consider that an awkward past has caused a difficult challenge in the present. Some people feel they cannot run from challenging elements that are products of their history. They may think they are committed and can do nothing.

To change the past is impossible and in the realm of fantasy. Therefore, we cannot raise our fists heavenwards to demand a clean slate. Instead, we can take comfort by believing that whatever happened would not have happened if it were not feasible in the order of things.

It is seldom accepted or understood that we can be challenged, acquire learning, and have direction from a 'bad' experience. Instead, it sounds better to say, 'We must tackle problems, learn from our experience, and strive to improve,' which is the same thing.

Pause a moment to recall the three most dreadful things in your life. Once you have done this, think next of the three most wonderful things. Now read the footnote[42]. Whatever the challenge, there is always something to be learned.

This learning is sometimes latent and actualizes later. Everything is a collection of experiences waiting for alignment. Nobody can explain how this happens. So, we need to be patient as we persevere. We will get to know when we keep ourselves open and ready.

* * *

Life is like the lifetime employment of old-world Japan. Either people find something to do, or they slowly but surely, opt out of the wheel of life. It is easy to consider this and say, 'How true,' sitting back on a comfortable chair, sipping a cup of coffee, electricity powering your house, and a major part of your lifetime ahead of you. However, it is *tough to accept a purpose for us to address.* Especially when we feel too old to change.

We, young and old, can find many things requiring attention. Still, we simply fail to personalize such requirements due to perceived limitations. Many would claim, 'That's not my job' instead because their ego cannot accept a purpose they have not created.

Everything is a chore when one has not discovered one's aim in life, whatever the stage of it. If we feel we lack direction, the remedy lies in choosing challenges of interest and adopting these challenges as part of our purpose.

Life is not about letting it slip by but doing what we can when we can. Of course, you may get results immediately, a year from now, or ten years later. But, when we recognize and *accept* our purpose in the present,

---

42 Which came easier? The negative is generally more likely. We do remember our lessons.

we will attract the things that overcome the past and help fulfill this purpose.

This may seem magical, but it is not. You are more likely to notice what can help you progress when focused on a purpose. As a result, you get into the flow more readily. First, accept the facts. Second, influence what you can to make it better.

Some challenges, like Alzheimer's, seem to border on inexplicable cruelty. Can anybody ever develop the empathy necessary to get inside the heads of those who face such challenges?

We find stories of remarkable courage among those who choose to share their experience. Yet, their core is impenetrable. Hidden in their pain, affliction, or condition could be awareness and sensitivity far beyond anything any ordinary person can realize.

Some might feel that being singled out or the isolation they experience is unfair, but all of us, the ordinary and the challenged, live in separate personal worlds. There is no complete understanding of one another. Still, we can reach out. We are often surprised when we do reach out eventually.

Challenges such as unfortunate experiences, disease, and disability could exist to encourage us as a race to reach out to one another. It's a lesson in tough love from the cosmos and creation.

* * *

Enlarging our concerns and donning a more significant role in what concerns us makes personal purpose evident. In this role, we learn to distinguish a life well rewarded from a rewarding life. Once we discover such a distinction between *material* and *existential* rewards, we can anchor firmly in life.

So, be grateful for your progress and the rewarding insights you accrue as you accept challenges and define your purpose. Challenge is a navigator when viewed with the proper perspective.

Life is not the world of Sartre or the world of a mad scientist with your brain hooked into some 'reality machine.' The world is yours. If you can think, use it. If you can move, use it. If you can see it, use it. If you can talk, use it. You will walk the path of our species and society as you do your unique and personal *walk of life*. You are living for yourself and your concerns. *Carpé Diem*. Seize the day.

If we recognize our personal progress, our sense of wellness endures. Therefore, the third mantra from the book for you to adopt is a 'gutsy' vital principle, *'Know [your] betterment in every circumstance.'* Emblazon this in your mind as well.

* * *

This is all okay for a younger person, some would say. The feeling of gradual betterment may be natural when you are young. However, Nachiket projected into the future when he asked how people could be proactive when older. Their strength and mental abilities get worse, not better.

We can offset growing older to an extent. It is never too late to learn new skills. Find that quality that brings your years of living into sharp focus. This is the difference between having five years of experience, ten times around, or discovering that you have fifty years of novel experience.[43]

---

43 See Appendix section "Find Gold in Old."

CHAPTER 10

TRADITION

'My problem is not with my delusions now, but with some actions in the past that I now regret. For instance, I feel guilty about transgressing some religious beliefs. What I experienced is retribution for this.' Nachiket said, indicating he needed further explanations.

Dharmaraj responded, 'Religion is always personal. A personal choice should dictate the extent of your religious beliefs and the practice of these beliefs. It may not always be feasible to stick to all religious practices in our humdrum world. Still, we need not feel guilty.'

'Religion dictates so much ritual and protocol. Religion and its rituals must have a purpose. These tenets could not have been handed down blindly from generation to generation,' said Nachiket.

'You could be right,' conceded the doctor. 'However, it is useful to remember that they were handed down from ages past and are dissimilar in different faiths. There is no commonality in ritual. Yet, every religion does provide existential explanations as a safety net before we can rely on our competence. For many, if it were not for religion, all would be bleak until they discover their own hope and motivation. Religion provides purpose until purpose becomes your religion.'

'Are the several claims of an ultimate human fate, self-realization, or heaven and hell just imaginary?' Nachiket asked, expressing a common doubt.

'Not necessarily,' said the doctor, again choosing his words carefully. 'All I am saying is living that aligns oneself; our personal life, work, and community is best. Our ultimate destination need not concern us now. Living a life of reasonable and constructive choices today without feeling anxious about an ultimate reward and punishment is all that matters.

If states like enlightenment exist, they are beyond current understanding. So, we need not be apprehensive of the unknown and follow religious beliefs out of fear or guilt. We can do so by choice. By the same license, we can also choose to debunk the entire religious razzmatazz if we find it unhelpful.'

'What if I choose but cannot follow everything?' queried Nachiket.

'There is still no need for guilt,' the doctor said emphatically. 'If you follow a reasonable, constructive, and personal purpose, there can be no wrongdoing. When you begin to believe in a progressive mission, unique yet shareable, the mission enables you to make the right choices. Hence, your actions spontaneously align with a purpose.'

Nachiket began to get agitated. 'My guilt is beyond anything you can understand. Religion is just a part of it. You can't imagine what I have done to others around me because of my callous attitude! I used to feel I was not answerable for anything I did. But now that I am awake to true reality, there seems to be a lot to regret.'

A tear rolled down Nachiket's cheek. The doctor felt this could be the turning point. Finally, Nachiket was ready to understand something bothering him deep down in a new light. Dharmaraj extended and placed his hand on Nachiket's. 'You can tell me about it. I am with you.'

Nachiket spoke with a catch in his throat. 'I have done many things that are plain wrong and have hurt numerous people. How do I come to terms with these deeds? I missed so many relationships that could have been fulfilling. You tell me this is all fated. In that case, I would be the unluckiest person alive.

Before telling him how much I loved and admired him, I lost my father. I lost a girl I doted on when I got the disability. Some of my deeds seem outrightly perverse. I feel I was thoughtless in many ways. I abused so many others. Now that I am recovering, I should feel better, but I feel terrible. How could I have been that way? Now I can never go back to correct what went wrong.'

It was a cathartic release, and the doctor spoke kindly. 'Underlying forces over which you had no control influenced you. Do not blame yourself for this. What's done is done and belongs in the past. Love only goes when it wants to teach you to love better.

I am afraid no technique can make good the loss of a love or mend broken relationships from the past. All you can do is build good memories from this point on. You should not see the future as an extension of your history. So let me share some ideas on coping with regret and loss.'

The doctor highlighted some points to help Nachiket tackle his sense of loss[44].

Nachiket then grew composed. 'I am sorry,' he said, wiping his tears and sitting up straight.

'Don't feel bad,' said the doctor reassuringly. 'Expressing valid emotions is not wrong. If I know you, you have made up your mind. Of course, you can explore emotions fully, but you also need to let go of what is not relevant for today....'

'I feel much better now. It is as if a weight has lifted,' said Nachiket.

'It is common to attribute everything bad to oneself alone,' the doctor explained. 'Instead, treat your past, good or bad, as fate. As things slip into the past, they no longer have full power. You can now make proactive choices and face up to whatever is ahead.

---

44 See RI 5 *"Beginning to Start Over"* at the end of the book under Recovery
    Instruments

You must trust time to heal any limitations you still feel. Stand up and be counted among those who grasp life with confidence. You have it in you.'

'I know what I must do, and I can do it. Is there anything else you have to say or anything we have left unexplored?' Nachiket looked at the doctor squarely.

'Nothing!' exclaimed the doctor. 'Go ahead and grab your new life with enthusiasm. I know a perfect counselor who will be able to help you manage habitual discouraging thoughts. Take these meetings as the last miles in your recovery.'

'Can I come and see you whenever I want?' asked Nachiket.

'You only need to see me as a friend, not a doctor. Write to me.' The doctor smiled. 'We will keep in touch to ensure all remains well and for your prescriptions. I wish you the very best!'

Dr. Dharmaraj had not been the typical psychiatrist, just prescribing medication and waiting for the cessation of symptoms. He had acknowledged that the larger world was not perfect, which is evident to most of us. We continue, nonetheless.

Nachiket had felt his capacity to tackle his surroundings was inadequate. He adopted his peculiar outlook to work around the distress he felt. So, he fabricated an unstable mental sanctuary to try and protect himself.

Dharmaraj had crossed over to Nachiket's world and looked outward with him, sitting by his side. He had not confronted him or tried to disprove his delusions logically. Instead, he waited for Nachiket to gain insight, nudging his thoughts and removing his fears.

A whole, but timid persona, dwelled within Nachiket, waiting to feel free. If Nachiket could only take ownership of his life, he would be safe. He could even be among the 40 percent afflicted who get back to the mainstream.

Though Nachiket seemed less confident now than before, Dr. Dharmaraj reassured the parents that his inner strength had grown. Instead of hiding in an artificial cocoon of false beliefs, he was ready to face his fears and make considerable strides in his personal well-being.

The doctor found that the initial push to stability with short-term medication was sometimes enough for some. However, the doctor insisted that Nachiket should keep taking his medication. For now, medication was Nachiket's lifeline to reality.

To tackle Nachiket's discouraging thoughts that continued despite his understanding, the doctor referred Nachiket to a counselor. What remained was to change some ways of harmful thinking that had become a habit.

BATON OR VAULTING POLE

Section Highlights

- Among the aspects that could affect our outlook are traditional beliefs and their physical, intellectual, and emotional impact.
- Traditional beliefs could be essential foundations for forming one's own unique worldview.
- The extent to which we conform to traditional beliefs and practice rituals should result from personal choice. Force, fear, or hype cannot be the basis.
- When we nurture and celebrate bettering Creation in any way or form, we can be guiltless and feel abundant, whatever the extent of our explicit traditional practice.
- If we don a responsibility to improve our world, as supporters of tradition or otherwise, we can transcend meaningless conflict.

Why did Nachiket find it necessary to discuss tradition and then his relationships? Traditions cause confusion in two areas: One, ritualistic practices celebrating God, and Two, roles and relationships between and among genders. Conflicts in these often trigger episodes of crisis in schizophrenia patients[45]. Here are some explanations for settling to rest some of the disputes.

Traditions form a significant part of our historical learning. However, many cultural beliefs and practices may seem confusing, sometimes even brutal, to sensitive schizophrenia patients.

Should we then conclude that all tradition is unviable with no role in the present? Should we challenge history and our interpretations of what is moral or immoral? A rational explanation for our traditional leanings and relationships, rendered outside traditional bounds and blind faith, will help.

* * *

Traditional thinking affects everybody, whether we are followers or not. Some social factions declare that traditional rituals, handed down over the ages, are mandatory for balanced living. Such diktats are a part of the collective mnemonic too. Many of us adopt an unquestioning belief to the extent that we feel uneasy and fearful if we skip traditional rituals.

Elders state that there are reasons for these practices and that questioning them is blasphemy. Still, for some, following traditional beliefs, customs, and rituals, or avoiding them, could be like trying to leap backward or forward in understanding. I say that because the question of which state is better is wide open.

The best state is a stable state. But then, stability in a traditional outlook requires an initial commitment by us, with some degree of intellectual or emotional dedication. Only then can it be without conflict. Dr. Dharmaraj does not say it in so many words, but this is his point. He

---

45 Crisis episodes, in the case of schizophrenia, are a sudden precipitation of symptoms including blatant displays of odd behavior

wants Nachiket to be comfortably stable with his level of traditional practice.

Tradition, particularly religion, is in our roots, and it is impossible to imagine a world without them. When people seek explanations, faith and religion attempt answers. The several explanations of Creation traditionally provided often function as support systems in our upbringing.

Sometimes, they seem illogical, but we follow them as they are comforting. Most beliefs intend to safeguard, just as a child's crib is meant to protect, not imprison. Or, they can perhaps be the scaffolding that helps us construct a personal worldview.

The basis for Nachiket's delusion was a belief in the existence of a supreme state and rebirth. The mind cannot resolve the presence of a supreme being and a personal soul without bringing in all the associated baggage of spirits, demons, and demigods. If people can conceive of a God, why shouldn't we consider the rest? This leads us back to the magical-religious aspects of ritual—what it heralds or wards away.

With their associated symbolism, rituals can profoundly impact the psyche. For believers, it creates a helpful force within. It allows them to face the vagaries of life with levelheadedness and a sense of protection. Life spares the non-believers the entire paradigm. They just go about existing, praising, or blaming only themselves and the environment they experience. Hence, ambivalent feelings about ritual and tradition occur only for those stuck between believing and questioning.

For the unsure, as Nachiket was after he came out of his delusion, one can propose that we view Creation as a property of existence. Just as heat is a property of fire, Creation is a property of 'is-ness,' nothing more. Also, just as heat has something hot like a fire behind it, Creation is a manifestation of an *a priori* force.

Because we experience its manifestation, we can conclude there is a force, or a force behind a force, or a force behind a force behind a force, *ad infinitum*. In other words, because we cannot wish away this manifestation, we cannot wish away the existence of a power.

Therefore, there is a force, whatever the levels upon which it comes stacked. You could call this force Nature or call it God. It permeates all that is matter, energy, space, and time.

A rational argument favoring the possibility of God existing goes thus. The non-believers can only claim there *may not* be a God but cannot—and probably do not—claim there *is* no God. They cannot claim that God, defined in any manner, does not exist. This is because none of us have experienced all of time and space.

According to scientists, time is a dimension, which must mean that God might exist somewhere, at some time, and at the *same* time! Therefore, the absence of evidence is not evidence of absence[46]. This is a comforting thought for believers because this argument negates the God *does not exist* hypothesis while allowing for the rationalist's opinion: God *may not exist*.

However, most theological conflicts are not from such a core dichotomy of existence or the non-existence of God. Instead, they arise from interpretations portraying a 'God' with all the quirks of a mortal (for example, a jealous God).

Religious clashes, or claims by purists, that one point of view is superior to another seem licensed by the idea that God has mortal properties and expectations. The use of fear, force, or hype using such a God is the cause of much social unrest and conflict. One person's faith, or understanding, seems superstition or without logic to another.

Entire societies could base their functioning on values promoting one-upmanship and victory over other forms of understanding. For example, some interpret the Quran as declaring that true Islam cannot accept other religions. Some claim immigration officials of Islamic

---

46 Carl Sagan (1934–96)

countries search and destroy non-Islamic religious texts and pictures at entry.

How can we feel motivated in an obviously splintered world? How can we resolve conflicts in us that may arise from differences in the practices and teachings of different beliefs? How can we feel personally aligned in our outlook despite making dissimilar choices?

A simple test for our traditional personal style would be our comfort and personal resolve. For example, when a person performs the *Namaaz*, or a *Vedic* ritual, without coercion, it reflects the strength of personal commitment and subscription to his faith by the individual.

Hence, those practicing tradition and faith should be able to do so without the validation of others. Similarly, if people lack traditional beliefs, they need not convince others. We can achieve a personal, communal, or other meaningful goal feeling the same sense of commitment.

We can subsume the apparent conflicts amongst various schools of ideological thought with a personal commitment to the greater good. We can have different beliefs yet be humane, caring, and considerate to one another and our home in the cosmos. What we need to do, despite diverse views, is to nurture that which Is, in the way we want. Any belief or ritual that does not go against humane principles is likely to be civilized and valid.

Living can be guiltless if a person is bettering himself and being constructive as a believer or a non-believer. When we don this responsibility to make things better, we transcend conflict. Therefore, tradition is both a baton to pass on and a vaulting pole to release after we make the jump. Treat it suitably

THE SEXUAL SKIRMISH

Section Highlights

- Confusion on roles and relationships often blocks the discovery of our personal purpose.
- The confusion causes distressing thoughts of guilt prompted by standard definitions of immorality.
- All genders have a joint mission, so there is no need to jockey for superiority.
- Any relationship can endure if it is humane, caring, and not harmful.
- Negativity in relationships can be overcome by investing in commitment.

There is a delicate area in tradition with an awkward legacy within the collective mnemonic—that of gender roles and relationships. These sometimes contribute to the onset of schizophrenia and influence mental health.

In this section, I extend some cursory explanations on partnerships to try and help the afflicted and the sensitive resolve simple glitches in their relationships. The advice on relationships shared in the following paragraphs is very much in passing compared to specialized books on the topic.

The intent is to share information on maintaining relationships and outline its primary aspects. It cannot replace counseling but throws some light on more apparent relationship issues.

Stability in roles and relationships with a significant other, if that be our choice, is important for us to live our purpose. Delving deeper, Nachiket's relationships with key people in his life seemed to have also contributed to the onset of his condition. From the cathartic and emotional release in his meeting with Dharmaraj, Nachiket revealed he was disturbed by certain aspects of his relationships.

Nachiket was young, and the immature's tendency to mess around and/or idealize their relationship can take an emotional toll. Often, schizophrenia is precipitated in a sensitive person by the feeling that his relationships are being threatened by others or that they are immoral. In addition, conflicting social ideas on matrimony and confusion about sexual orientation may affect the psyche at its core.

* * *

A question - almost naïve: *Why are we two sexes?* Again, John and Mary Gribben, co-authors of the book, *The One Percent Advantage,* cited earlier, have also suggested an evolutionary basis for having two distinct sexes.

Consider the primordial 'ooze' of amino acids and other life-giving material that existed at one stage in the planet's history. An active, small cell can swim around rapidly in the primordial ooze and find a partner. However, because of its size, such a cell will not carry many 'resources' to nurse the next generation.

A big, fat cell will be an excellent provider of resources but will not be very mobile. When small cells meet and mate, other microbes may gobble up their even smaller offspring. Big, sedentary cells will not find a mate unless a small, mobile cell swims up to them.

Immediately we have the beginnings of a robust system of reproduction involving two sexes. A 'female' provides the large egg, and a 'male' contribution is a packet of genetic information and a map for the biological development of the lifeform.

The human lifeform is complex, and one sex with a long gestation period would have been incapable of propagating and evolving rapidly. Therefore, Nature provided another component unrestricted from reproduction during the gestation period. This unrestricted component also can produce both resource-providing and mobile elements. i.e., One sex can build both sexes by passing on the gene determining sex.

Voila—we have the female and male of the species. The evolutionary logistics of the complex human lifeform demanded two sexes. Nature provided this, equipping each sex with specific roles in propagation. There are two roles in biology, but one mission as a species. Our only mission as a species may be to stay on our mental and physiological evolutionary path.

* * *

Sexual Dimorphism, such as the difference in height between sexes, is an aspect in many species. The bigger the male is on average compared with the female of the species, the more the number of females, on average, in the male's harem.

In species that are monogamous, such as most birds, there is significantly less or no difference in size at all. Hence, the continuing disparity in size between men and women suggests a natural tendency towards polygyny in us. This means we already have natural drivers that test our commitment to monogamous human relationships.

Several social thinkers and lawmakers have advised marriage to prevent an emotional rupture between members. The need for an institution of marriage, in which laws support love, is a social construct to provide some security to relationships. Since wealth and its ownership are in the domain of law, it seems wise for both parties to take the shelter provided by this social construct.

But, when speaking with a liberal bent of mind, there is no need for a stamp of legal validity for one-on-one relationships to succeed. Perhaps we will one day evolve to a point where this issue is redundant. But, for now, marital security, monogamy included, seem necessary. The last I heard, marriage and/ or monogamy were still popular!

* * *

Next, can we argue that relationships must be free of gender-based jockeying? The delegation of genders to distinct social roles is the cause of discrimination and wars. But there is no need to prove one gender is mightier than the other.

Social roles today have enough proof that all genders have a joint mission. But having said that, we must be comfortable when our relationships do not conform to tradition. Unfortunately, because of outdated classic fiats, some conclude erroneously that certain relationships or practices are immoral.

Examples of non-traditional relationships are marriages with wide age differentials or relationships in which the women are significantly older. They could also be same-gender or inter-religious marriages (and others still lacking common social acceptance).

The individuals in such partnerships need intellectual and emotional acceptance for the relationship to succeed. Whatever the type of relationship, the commitment, caring, and compassion shared between the members determine its success. Any relationship that does not transgress civility and has the preceding qualities seems valid.

Those in relationships that lack widespread social approval had better be impervious to criticism. Times will change, but non-traditional relationships presently require great emotional maturity.

This advanced age proposes we must go beyond traditional gender roles. We must accept that two sexes exist originally because of a biological need, not a temperamental one. We must forget the skirmish of the sexes.

* * *

A relationship is always dynamic. It is an entity in motion. Hence, we need to maintain every relationship. A relationship can be likened to a virtual tank with a leak. We must keep filling it up with nurturing thoughts, words, and deeds.

When a serious personal intent to belong supports the relationship, maintaining it is a welcome task. Our choice to be in or out of a relationship endures successfully. The intention to belong drives us to do the right things in it.

Feelings of distrust, jealousy, and guilt can be overcome by devoting effort, caring, and commitment to our relationships. When we back the relationship with the strength of duty, we gladly invest in it. We learn to develop trust and fuel its success. First, commit love. The rest will follow.

* * *

DESTRUCTIVE SEXUAL ORIENTATION

A word in passing about unacceptable sexual orientations. Consider that sexual intimacy (and rape, at the other extreme), as opposed to recreational sex, automatically carries with it some emotional angles. It is a sharing (or breaching, in the case of rape) of trust that is very personal. We are right, therefore, in explicitly condemning those who seek relationships that transgress a sense of civility (such as in the case of pedophiles). But, on the other hand, when sex is caring and not based on destructive drivers, we can play out our choices without guilt.

A famous personality once said, 'I would rather be single [or in a relationship] for the right reasons than be with someone [or single] for the wrong ones.' Yet another quip, attributed to Socrates, is the last word on relationships. Despite its pessimism, it seems applicable to relationships of this age, [albeit with some modifications]: 'As to marriage [read: being in a relationship] or celibacy [read: being single], let a man [read: a person] take which course he [or she] will; he [or she] will be sure to repent it [every once in a while!]' [47].

* * *

---

[47] For further insights on relations between men and women, please read the classic by GRAY, JOHN. *Men Are from Mars, Women Are from Venus*: HarperCollins publishers, 1993

There is learning hidden in our failed emotional relationships, although it is learning that nobody consciously seeks. Learning from heartbreak and grief is virtually inevitable for all of us.

Nachiket's feelings of loss weighed heavily on him and compounded his illness. Sometimes we have time to prepare for our loss, but sometimes the triggering event, such as sudden death, is shattering.

In his book, Illusions, Richard Bach says, 'Here is a test to find whether your mission on earth is finished: If you're alive, it isn't.'[48] This may be the best consolation for us regarding the death of others - Their mission was complete[49].

48 Richard Bach in *Illusions – Adventures of a Reluctant Messiah* Dell Publishing Co., Inc. Publication (1977)
49 See Appendix section "Beginning to Start Over"

PART V: The Conclusion

The boy's academic test results were about average. He says, 'I knew this would happen, but is there a reason?'

The mentor explained, 'You must understand that you will do better if you practice and work at it long enough and hard enough. You must want it fiercely.'

The boy asks, 'How does this test judge that?'

'Well,' the mentor ventured, 'If you'd really wanted to do well in it bad enough, you would have worked hard for it.'

The boy smiles, 'So the test judged how much doing well in it meant to me.'

'Within reason... It may also have tested how long you wanted to succeed in it,' says the mentor.

'Whoa! Does that mean if I don't get around to wanting anything I desire well in time, it won't amount to much?' was the boy's wry question.

The mentor laughed, 'Yep. It is important to move on once you realize this. We shouldn't repeatedly try the same old keys on the same old doors. It will come to naught. Instead, you can be open to new chances for achievement and success.': *Anon*

CHAPTER 11

ARMOUR

Dr. Dharmaraj briefed a counselor on Nachiket's case and affliction. Even after coming to terms with his condition, Nachiket may habitually conjure harmful and discouraging thoughts. Therefore, the counselor would provide Nachiket with some techniques to neutralize negative thinking... unhealthy and unhelpful thinking.

After going through his background and present state, the counselor continued her discussion with Nachiket. 'Dr. Dharmaraj told me to help you with overcoming unhelpful thoughts. Are such thoughts triggered by memories?'

Nachiket replied, 'Not strictly memories. But, I find, they are often due to some judgments... my own and others.'

'Flawed thoughts come from certain habits we pick up early,' the counselor explained. 'The point then is to change the habits. But, first, recognize that the habit is not helpful. Then you can challenge it.'

'How?' Nachiket asked.' I am stuck replaying strings of flawed attributes in my head.'

'There is a systematic methodology to change this, which I will teach you. Positive but realistic self-talk and the steps we will discuss are often all that is needed. You can break bad thinking habits and build new ones that foster confidence.'

Over the next few meetings, the counselor walked Nachiket through the steps for handling random discouraging thoughts[50].

Once Nachiket got the hang of the technique, the counselor asked, 'Do you have any doubts?'

Nachiket was keen on getting his life back in order and countered, 'Do I need to know anything else?'

The counselor answered. 'Life is meant for you to do, learn and enjoy. As you go on, you will experience several unique incidents, some of which may test your limits. Don't get disheartened. You will learn everything you need from them. The learning never stops.

Learn from life and look beyond every setback. Your life will then be progressive and rewarding. The thing to understand is that emotions depend on thoughts. Change the thought, and you can change the emotion.

It needs some effort, but the technique is simple and really helps. If you keep applying it consciously, you can overcome the habit of thinking adversely,' reassured the counselor.

'Does this mean I can pursue a normal life? You know: academics, work, marriage, children...?' inquired Nachiket.

'I would say yes,' declared the counselor. 'There are certain things you learn only on the job. But I think the foundation is set, and you can venture to bigger things.'

After the last meeting with the counselor, she watched Nachiket as he walked away with a definite spring in his step. Nachiket turned back, saw her, and flashed a thumbs-up sign. The counselor smiled and returned the gesture.

---

50 See RI 6, *The Last Error*, in the Recovery Instruments section at the end of the book

Nachiket no longer felt discouraged when things did not go his way and always picked himself up. He spoke affirmations to himself. He continually challenged reactive negative thoughts and replaced them with helpful, proactive thinking. The words 'Change the thought, change the emotion' had charged Nachiket.

When the sessions with Dr. Dharmaraj and the counselor concluded, Nachiket felt as much in control as anyone normally would. He returned to his disrupted education and began working earnestly toward his goals. He felt the thrill of using his mind and achieving the goals that he set for himself. His unique learning provided a progressive perspective, a 'can do' attitude, and an unshakeable belief in *grace*. Nachiket knew there was no need to ponder whether such grace was divine or mundane.

FINAL ENABLERS

Section Highlights

- Cooperative reciprocity can be practically applied by being aware and mirroring actions.
- Acquiring the ability to empathize is an essential enabler for achievement.
- Focus on what you have instead of what is lost in your decisions.
- We need to handle vexatious people by being sufficiently detached and contextual.
- Anger may be a valid response when we are victims of unfair behavior or judgments.
- When nothing is going your way, be patient and receptive to change. Trust time to cradle you in its natural cycle.

We inevitably experience testing interactions with others and the environment. Therefore, we need to have specific skills and attitudes for being constructive in our interactions. To top off the ideas in the book, some suggestions that can help the afflicted or the diffident operate in the social mainstream are shared. In these last few sections of the book, we converge on a proactive mindset's final elements.

A book is never a replacement for practice. Still, the following paragraphs discuss some factors important for interacting in and with our world. These ideas can enhance our ability to function effectively in our personal and professional environments.

* * *

COOPERATIVE RECIPROCITY:

Cooperative reciprocity, as explored before, is a survival strategy based on Dr. Robert Trivers' work on the evolution of cooperation in a species[51]. It suggests, for best results, mimicking what the other person does, positive or negative, after offering collaboration at the beginning or commencement of the interaction.

How does cooperative reciprocity work? Be nice if they are nice. Do not be nice if they are not nice. This simple technique pays big dividends. This means whenever you approach anyone in the first instance with an issue, extend a hand of cooperation, then respond just as they act from that point on.

If they raise their voice, raise yours. If they use an obscene word, use one. If they ignore you, ignore them. However, if they move one step in your direction, move one step in theirs. If they use a conciliatory tone, do the same. If they alternate between cooperative and hostile positions, do the same, close on the heels of their action. Try it.

Please extend cooperation on every interaction's first or second instance despite any adverse move. Then, do just as the other person has done, *however*, in a manner that shows you care for the larger plan.

---

51 . The practical applications suggested here are the author's interpretation and not the views of Dr Trivers.

The art of cooperative reciprocity lies in picking the pivotal factor in the other person's actions or words and retorting with something similar. Remain focused on the context while you retort.

The next time you face negativity, pick the pivotal discomfiting factor (such as a gesture, a phrase, a tone, etc.). Then, think up a creative counter using that same trait (or its opposite) while sticking to the larger context. Again, the key is picking what you instinctively feel is transgression and retorting.

An example, if the other person just yelled, you could contrast powerfully by replying with a firm, steady tone. Extend cooperation once or twice more *before* you yell back. If the person acts like a jerk, you can contrast it by laughing. And, of course, you CAN get angry without losing control of the emotion. We'll talk about anger shortly.

You may be able to use cooperative reciprocity in any interaction, but with these caveats.

Caveat #1: Modify the intensity of reciprocation to suit the protocol of the situation. For example, the way to interact one-on-one may not be the same as in the presence of a third party.

Caveat #2: Offer out-of-the-way cooperation only when in an enduring relationship. Such exceptional collaboration pays off only with continuing opportunities for interactions in the future.

Caveat #3: Don't forsake extending cooperation, care, or compassion for the ones who deserve it, despite interactions that are rare or one-time.

EMPATHY:

An essential aid in interaction is empathy. But unfortunately, the push for it has become quite a cliché. But, of course, clichés become clichés because they have some truth. When appropriately practiced, empathy works to build bridges between people, except when it comes to the die-hard and opinionated.

Nevertheless, before we conclude that we have tried and failed, even with such people, empathy deserves full consideration. A villain, too, may have excellent excuses to be villainous.

Empathy, as you know, is seeing things from the other person's point of view. The definition is easy enough but implementing it is another story. So how do we empathize? Here are some pointers.

The first step towards empathizing is to respect others who have independent wishes, ideas, and needs, even though we may not subscribe to them. That is, we appreciate that different backgrounds lead to different understandings. When you recognize and celebrate that you are unique, it will be a small jump to acknowledge that others are too.

Next, it is important to listen. Often, when we let the other person have their FULL say, a different picture emerges, and we can see reasons for people to feel the way they do. In fact, they would realize the flaws in their reasoning or emotions when you provide them with supportive listening. If instead, we attack or attempt rationality before hearing people out, they may become defensive or hostile.

Further, *we* can do some things to make the *other* person open and be more empathetic.

To do this, first, avoid commenting on their personality. For example, avoid crass phrases such as, 'Your careless attitude makes me angry,' or 'I hate it when you act cool.' Characteristics could be in-built. How people contribute to the circumstances and context, not their personality, matters.

Second, avoid rhetorical questions. For example— 'Why are you so forgetful?' or 'Why are you always late?' There are no answers to such questions. If you need to know more, ask open-ended questions.

Third, establish that you are trying to understand. Again, the best thing is to be explicit about this by saying something like 'I am trying to understand, but I am confused,' or 'What you say will make more sense to me if you explain a little more.'

Finally, nobody will understand your personal or professional effort if *you* haven't figured out what you are doing. You control this aspect of empathy. Hence, make sure you thoroughly understand what you want to accomplish. Then, others will be disposed to accept it.

You do not need to travel the whole distance for a sense of clarity. Instead, like driving a car with headlights, be clear about what is in your immediate visibility. You will then travel the whole way, a little at a time.

The last thought on empathizing. When an individual passionately subscribes to an idea, although it is patently wrong, you cannot persuade the person. In such instances, the best thing to do may be to use an external influencer. Or, walk away until a better time or wait till the person discovers their folly on their own. Sometimes it is the most empathetic thing to do.

DECISIONS:

Most choices we must make are not as dire as deciding which of the twins gets a seat in the lifeboat. But, agreed, most of us have faced tough choices that could have led to regret.

Should I send that money for my father's medication or pay my mounting credit card debt? Do I put my aged dog to sleep or continue caring for her until she dies? Do I risk being unprepared for my meeting early tomorrow by helping my son with his math quiz? It seems evident that something must give.

Most decisions, however, are much simpler than a seat in a lifeboat. You can get away with few regrets, whatever the consequence. However, occasionally, a situation requires a leap of faith that you could regret later. So how do you choose and unequivocally accept that choice for the long run?

Experience is the way you use your yesterday. You know that rationally, but you also must trust time to emotionally heal the impact of a wrong decision. The more you focus on the sacrifice (or mistake), the more you focus on loss. The more you focus on what you have now, the more you focus on your learning (or growth).

It helps to believe that all your choices, before this point, have facilitated your learning. What you have is the raw material with which you can build. When you use your experience, you are aware of the *you* that has taken shape—the person you are today. Be true to that person.

VEXATIONS:

The comfort you feel with your decisions and choices will invariably be disturbed. Genuine arguments and disagreements do not cause this disturbance. These usually have rational resolutions. Real vexations are from the subtle ridicule, unfair arm-twisting, or other forms of power-play that sometimes occur in social interactions.

For some, these power plays are a way of life. They move on, inexorably trampling sentiment, decency, and dignity. They may be blissfully unaware that they have compromised another's self-esteem or triggered discontent.

We can only guess why some individuals behave in a vexatious manner. Their position is tenuous without props; they suffer from inadequacy or have ambitions built on relative worth. You cannot address most of the reasons, so do not try to change these individuals. It will only add to your vexation.

Please understand that you cannot avoid politically motivated pressure. We cannot always react to put-downs, verbal-jousting or psychological ploys used by some people. We must therefore learn to manage the vexations we face. We can read the signs and take steps to be poised.

How? Firstly, the most crucial factor in handling vexatious people is to be sure you are right. This breed can sense uncertainty like a dog can sense fear. Once they know you are unsure, a steamroller of heavy-handed statements emerges.

Hence, before you take up an issue with this group of people, ensure you are correct, and all your ducks lined up. Do your homework.

Second, it is helpful to remember the recent history of your interactions with them. They take advantage of the forgetfulness of others. They may confuse, contort, and lie without tangible proof of their earlier assurances.

Therefore, you must consciously remember and record your interactions if you want to progress with this breed.

Finally, be detached from the issue or any of its aspects. People attached to an issue focus on defending their turf instead of a larger relevant agenda. We are likely to be reactive instead of proactive when attached. Emotional attachment can make us miss some salient points.

Your passion has its place but cannot replace your presence of mind. Concentrate on the context. Be in the moment.

ANGER:

Most anger is a by-product of envy, impatience, or relative worth. A brief exploration of the emotion of anger will help us understand its adverse effects while highlighting why it is sometimes valid.

We will lose our temper when others push our buttons, deliberately or otherwise. It's debatable, but anger is often personal. It does not purely come from disagreement with an idea or event. On the contrary, we are patient with those we like, even in dispute.

There is something in the individual that we cannot tolerate triggering anger in us. Irritation usually does not result from a rational process of disagreement. Most people only work out the cause *after* they have blown their cool.

Nonetheless, not all anger is bad. I venture that losing your temper can be good in some situations. This emotion is destructive only when you lose it without control. When you lose self-control, the damage you can cause is sometimes irreparable.

Losing your temper can be good when it is a conscious release. In other words, when you base your resentment or frustration on facts, and when the situation can do with escalation, it could be wise to display your temper. It can be a valid response to unjust, flagrant, or aggressive transgressions—wrongdoings that invite no debate about their illegitimacy.

When people tell you to control your temper, never confuse it with valid anger. When you use it with care, anger can be a powerful ally to call upon in times of conflict. The knack ensures you are in control, channeling all the energy from the emotion. Then, you can choose to get angry when anger is appropriate.

DIFFICULTIES:

When you hit a low, or you feel none of your work is bearing fruit, or when you think you cannot try anymore, the tide will turn. Be patient.

It is the rule of the cosmos that things move in cycles. There are things you can never understand, and it is best to bide your time. Acknowledging this human fate is difficult. We feel frustrated at such times and seek a way out, hammering against the rock-solid walls of circumstance and inner limitations.

You can hammer away, but you will only hurt yourself more. The natural cycle of life will instead cradle you and lift you over time. When you recognize this, you realize that nothing about your moods or situation is permanent. There will be times when you feel good and others when you feel low. Meanwhile, be patient.

Funnel any disturbing energy in you into something creative. For example, write a letter to yourself or someone you feel you must express yourself, or sculpt something. There is no need to post the letter or show the sculpture. It is meant for merely letting out your feelings. If you have no one to write to, write to whatever power you believe in. You can let the darkness go out of you by your expression.

A sense of hopelessness may lock in some of us in our low times. Yet, creativity, such as writing or sculpting, can relieve us and provide hope.

Have faith that something is conscious of your creative effort, within you or outside of you. Someone in you is watching— your subconscious. Something in the cosmos is always witnessing. These work in mysterious ways to dissipate harmful energies and give you a new course and direction. Meanwhile, be patient.

Often, we just fail to ask. We forget that the squeaky wheel gets the grease. After thinking over and framing your requirements, approach those who can help. Refuse to let the box limit you. Help is available, professionally and personally.

Sometimes just visiting the library or spending a little time browsing the Internet would help you locate the assistance you need. Sow as many seeds as possible. Some will grow into saplings. Nurture the ones that grow carefully, as they could bear fruit. Meanwhile, be patient.

* * *

The ups and the downs in life pass practical learning on to us. It is hard when the downs are great adversities or prolonged states of sadness. When this happens, trust time. It will give you results appropriately. However, it may come to you in disguise.

When we are looking for physical comfort, we could get emotional growth. When we search for emotional solace, we may find an intellectual treasure; or when we seek wisdom...we find love.

Be open to learning whatever the past teaches, and surely, you will grow. Believe there is always improvement from this point forward, and surely, you will find it. Summing up, be ready to receive abundance *in any form*, and surely, you will have it.

It may be under several layers, but you can realize there are some things to be grateful for, whatever your circumstances.

You could be grateful that you are whole in limb, that your relationships are supportive, that you ate yesterday, that you still sleep, that you are sane, and so on. There are reasons to be grateful today, however insufficient your past has been and how distant your dreams may seem.

The next chapter stitches together the elements that make for a new outlook. Such an outlook bolsters our self-esteem... always.

CHAPTER 12

RESOLUTION

(A peek into Nachiket's journaling)

I have come a long way from believing I am a mythological persona. Now, I am trying to be rational. What I have to say might be hard to digest.

Many claim the ultimate refuge for us is religion. But most people today adopt religion to escape accountability or because they are superstitious and afraid to be without its support. As a result, they are often not practitioners by faithful, independent choice.

Some even follow a religion because they believe in returning to the 'glory' days—when their religion was indisputable. The moderate few are also emotionally inclined towards faith rather than persuaded by rationality.

Religion provides emotional solace but fragile logic. When one thinks about it, misinterpreted religion has divided societies and been the basis for several uncivilized acts.

We cannot rely on any single template that declares what is required because a single template cannot celebrate all beliefs in our world. Religion might need modulating by civilized reason.

What is the promise of religion that people realize when they practice it? The purpose of spiritual life, many believe, is self-realization, Godhead, Heaven, or Enlightenment. These are commonly claimed as our ultimate goals. Religion claims one can achieve a state of perfection or some ultimate form.

A vast plethora of gurus and religious leaders provide analyses of complex holy texts towards this end. Unfortunately, their clarifications of our ultimate goal are perfunctory and poetic because they are trying to describe a sensation of supreme divinity beyond life. Unfortunately, these 'teachers' tend to tell you that you have something lacking that can be filled only by the divine.

If you are a lover of verse, the beauty of these words may leave you spellbound. Moreover, it can make you thirst for a state of perfection with unsurpassed enthusiasm. But, all the while, this reinforces the idea that what you are is not enough.

There are several paradoxes in religion. Trying logic on these paradoxes often leads to a dead end. Too much introspection may trigger psychological side-effects or mental disabilities and hamper effective functioning in everyday life. We would go mad.

Are such states just a rosy promise? Is it pointless and wishful, then? 'Living happily' can be real when we debunk any obsession with Nirvana, Heaven, and such endpoints. Instead, we can go about our lives with any ideology that is caring and compassionate.

I now understand that we may decay and disintegrate in social goals if we forsake the immediate here and now for that which is outside the experienced. Our objectives must be tangible and real for us to belong and feel motivated. We need to scale down any huge spiritual endgame to be in the here and now.

Nirvana, Godhead, Self-realization, or Heaven, by its very definition, is impractical. The mind is capable of conceiving and describing these states poetically. Still, it cannot experience such conditions in its current limited form. Since, by definition, such an experience would have to be all-encompassing, there would be no palpable direction even if we end up in it.

Despite all I have read, I should not look for a state of all-pervading omniscience and everlasting bliss. All-pervading and eternal happiness, completeness, and super-consciousness, if they exist, are not teachable or acquirable using our current faculties simply because they are without measure. If it exists, the experience happens by *grace*.

I can only pray for that grace—physical, emotional, intellectual, and spiritual, to enter my experience. For me, the Big One can wait (or should I say, I can wait for the Big One).

Nachiket

CLARITY IN CONTROL

Section Highlights

- What we can influence, what we are concerned about, and what we depend on should take a descending order in the magnitude of their impact.
- Such a sequence in impact can ensure we are without harmful anxiety and remain motivated.
- Whether this is consistently so or not, we should accept the situation and try to retain or regain balance.
- We can retain or regain balance by creating mental, menial, or material value for others and ourselves.

Control. How much we desire control! We seek control over our work and its results, desires, relationships, and living in general. Our balance, poise, positive sense, and our ability to be proactive all seem to depend on the extent of our being in control. But, of course, things do not always go as planned. Murphy's Law[52] crops up in several of our activities.

Why is it difficult to be calm and proactive when facing challenges to our sense of control? What is the ideal outlook that can keep us worry-free?

---

52 Anything that can go wrong, will go wrong

We must understand that happy medium of existence where we can manage our degree of control without anxiety. The final ideas in the book are about consolidating its message and setting new terms to live by in our worlds.

* * *

Think of your actions in any situation as playing out from three overlapping virtual spheres. The three spheres are the individual's circles of influence, concern, and dependence (Pic. 4—*Spheres in our Decision Space*). We make decisions and respond based on the largest sphere in our situation[53].

Pic 4. Spheres in our Decision Space

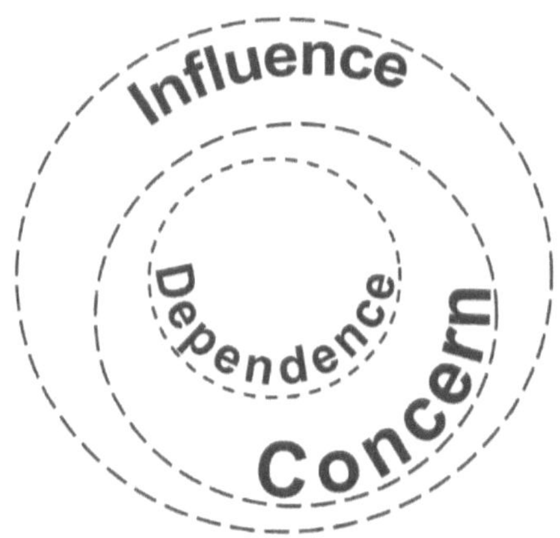

If pressures of social protocol from our being dependent forces our hand, we make compromises. We feel frustrated when our concerns involve things we cannot do anything about. In addition, if we cannot influence the things we think we should be able to, we may feel inadequate.

We cannot do away with the spheres that affect our sense of poise, but we can learn how to manage them.

---

53 Stephen Covey originally conceived a similar analysis.

Obviously, we must shrink the sphere of our dependence to the greatest possible degree. When you exhaust the transient props that support you and replace them, to the extent possible, with enduring ones, this sphere shrinks.

The next sphere, the circle of concern, is our source of motivation. Concern cannot manifest itself without interest, and interest cannot come without involvement. So, if you feel unconcerned today, become involved. Involvement is what motivates you and gets you into the mainstream.

Some view a job purely as a source of income—they cannot be motivated for long. But, if we learn more about our company: its stakeholders, fellow employees, the business functions and aims, we can become involved. We will get drawn into the mainstream as we get interested in the bigger picture.

It is necessary to stay concerned about a more comprehensive set of issues than only things we depend on. Therefore, our circle of concern must be of a size that includes a broader set, a set that would motivate us. However, these concerns should ideally be within what we can influence.

Anybody can stay concerned with one's life, at the very least. However, our circle of influence will be small if we look at life only in this way. So how do we increase our impact on the things that concern us? How can this influence stretch beyond a concern for oneself alone?

Adding value is the only way to increase the size of your sphere of influence. When we act on opportunities to add value to others, we invariably add value to ourselves. Your value addition requires some action—mental, menial, or material. It requires effort.

As discussed in the *Bona Fide Battle* section, the result or value depends on intent. A committed intent, which aims at contributing to a larger order, will unleash the required effort.

How do we develop this intent? How do we ensure relevance and continuity in value delivery and influence? How do we get involved gladly?

This is in the next Section.

THE VALUE VENUE

Section Highlights

- With focused efforts, small and large, we can ensure value creation.
- When we personalize and have empathy, our focus grows sharper. We clearly understand what value to deliver.
- A sense of ownership for the venues where we deliver value lends motivation, drives effort, and leads to satisfying and worthwhile results.
- If we cannot respect our current situation enough to feel motivated, we must search and choose what can command our respect.

It is exceedingly important to know what we can and cannot influence. *Whatever does not have a solution within what you can control cannot be your problem.* Sure, you could contribute in a roundabout way, but the problem is somebody else's.

While we know problems exist, they may also be givens about which you can do precious little.

Therefore, you should accept your existence 'as-is where-is' as suggested earlier in *The Nascent Notion*. Accept your challenges and reach out, as explained in *The Hidden Navigator*. When we are sure of what is personally possible and motivated by it, all unnecessary tension and anxiety drop off, well... at least for the better part.

As I tried to reinforce many times over, in various places in the book, you will find you can achieve more when you dedicate yourself to something more significant. You will unleash an unmatched drive when you wholeheartedly choose to serve something larger in time, place, and perspective.

The way to establish ourselves in a personally purposeful and value-creating journey is merely to begin. Even the worthless or shabby can turn into something excellent with solid intent. Create the value that contributes to getting better with small steps. Pat yourself on the back for *whatever* you can do.

To deliver value effectively and efficiently, we need to make *efforts*, *personalize* the interests of others, and take *ownership* of our tasks with dedication.

The effort suggested is an aspect of value that ensures one can 'perspire' and achieve. It removes any need to be born gifted or to be a genius to get extraordinary results. The effort here is old-fashioned hard work. However, we would not call it 'work' when it deals with what we are concerned about (our only obligations).

Imagine you had to fill in a database of 1,000,000 records (names and addresses, etc.). Not knowing when you were likely to finish, you apportioned your and your team's time and worked doggedly for days. Then, a database file that was only a fraction of a gigabyte began to grow. You got an archiving program and began backing it up on multiple media. You also made a copy on a mirrored server. You set up automatic backups and strict risk-mitigation measures against loss as the database grew and grew.

The end was slowly becoming a reality. Then, one morning, you uploaded the database to your client's server. You never knew (and will never know) its usage. But that instant when the upload was completed, and you received the closing payment was worth it all.

How is this valuable to you, leaving the payment aside? The real question to consider is, *are you better in one manner or another?* We usually are when we add value. In this case, you would have become more seasoned in your data storage and management skills. You learned while you earned.

Respect small efforts as much as the big ones. We need *not* wait for 'judgment day' to recognize what we are doing as worthwhile. Whatever you are doing is valuable if it is getting better and better every day *in some manner.* Every joy is multi-fold when we have worked hard without expecting miracles because the moment of achievement then *just happens.*

Many negligible small acts would magically transform into an excellent result. In the humility of the doer to take small steps lies the ability to achieve big results. If you respect the littlest effort, wasted or otherwise, a payoff is inevitable. A gain for what you are working towards... often. A gain for yourself... every time! Remember, our abilities, knowledge, and wisdom keep growing.

This brings us to the second driver for effectiveness in value delivery after the vital ingredient of effort. You must *personalize.* Think of personalization as a selfless effort for personal betterment. This seeming contradiction can be a revelation. It is about letting go of the minor ego for a bigger self.

Personalization means: To have a personal yet broad empathetic perspective. This cannot happen unless you practice being inclusive. One needs to include the interests of others. We have already discussed empathy, but its importance cannot be understated. Empathize with your spouse and kids, and you have a happy family. Empathize with your boss and customers, and you have an excellent job. Empathize with the community and the world to become a contributing citizen.

After effort and personalization, our sense of ownership is the final driver to delivering value. This refers to a sense of belonging to our chosen value venue.

Ownership involves respect on an institutional scale. We cannot truly belong to an institution we disrespect. You can do more by respecting it, whether a job or a relationship.

Ownership happens with a symbiosis between the individual and the *process*. This occurs when a two-way flow of value between the person and the process of achievement takes place. The symbiotic relationship will ensure learning or some other gain for you, tangible or intangible. At the same time, the process goes towards a specific result: personal, professional, or social. So, there's value for the venue where results are delivered. At the same time, it contributes to your evolution.

* * *

These concluding thoughts on control and value should get you up and running with your personal purpose. However, suppose you feel you still cannot do this effectively in your situation. In that case, you may need to arm yourself with new goals that can help in a two-way flow of value between you and what concerns you.

If we have no options to change things, it might be time to develop respect, beyond acceptance, for our condition. It is not a problem. It is the truth.

Try a different approach. Invest your effort, personalization, and ownership wisely and wait for gratification. Invest expecting returns later. If you seek or want to bring about change, search and choose what you can respect.

BEING HERE NOW

You should be able to link the ideas presented so far with three concepts, which the book offers as its keystones. The crux of the personal success the book expounds on is in understanding and applying this triad. Once grasped, these 'mantras' enable a personal acceptance of existence and its purpose.

The three 'mantras' are:

1. Meet your fate; make your destiny.
2. Realize your absolute, non-relative, and unique standing.
3. Know [your] betterment, or improvement, in every circumstance.

The first of the triad *Meet your fate; make your destiny*, reflects an attitude that helps us accept our situation while maintaining control. We can interpret fate as what we meet and destiny as what is created by how we meet fate.

There is no way out if we remain in denial or apathy. So instead, embrace the here and now. This is accepting fate. Taking control requires a firm resolve to be a value creator at the center of your life. That's how you carve your destiny.

It is never too late. Do not question your fate. Act on your destiny. You will progress if you understand the ideas and apply the basic set of enablers shared.

The second part of the triad, *Realize your absolute, non-relative, and unique standing*, is an attitude that drops jealousy, envy, and the blame-game.

Your standing is unrelated to any pecking order. We know social structures are needed in the management of civilized life. These will make some demands on you purely for the sake of protocol. However, these demands can be readily accepted if, at your core, you realize what a unique creation *you* are, as is *everybody* else.

Be proud of what you are and what you achieve. Be anchored in the uniqueness that is YOU.

The third, and last part of the triad, *Know [your] betterment, or improvement, in every circumstance*, relates to the path of constant growth, learning, and wisdom.

The consequences of our actions could be positive or negative. Still, once we realize everything contributes to personal progress, we would take what comes our way with a degree of composure. Every instance can be seen as an opportunity to grow.

We can be detached and poised in testing times while waiting for the tide to turn. Even in the most dismal of circumstances, if we can accept and adapt, we will walk away with the confidence to face a new day.

Maybe just a little or slowly, but you get to appreciate that things improve... even perpetually!

Our 'Bill of Rights,' suggested by Dr. Jerilyn Ross (1946–2010), is reproduced below. Dr. Ross was a pioneer and expert on therapies for anxiety disorders. She was co-author, with Rosalynn Carter, of the book *Triumph Over Fear*. This Bill of Rights is reassuring because it tells us it is okay to be human. It seems enough to seek life, one small step at a time. You just need to get started on it. Consciously.

BILL OF RIGHTS

- *I have the right to say No without feeling guilty*
- *I have the right to do what will make me happy if it does not infringe on another person's rights*
- *I have the right to ask for help*
- *I have the right to feel angry*
- *I have the right to feel confused*
- *I have the right not to care [worry]*
- *I have the right to offer no excuses for my behavior*
- *I have the right to have my needs respected*
- *I have the right not to know the answer*
- *I have the right to disagree*
- *I have the right to be weak*
- *I have the right to make a mistake and be responsible for it*
- *I have the right to cry*
- *I have the right to be scared*
- *I have the right not to like everybody*
- *I have the right to get what I pay for*

- *I have the right to ask for what I want, knowing that I can be refused*
- *I have the right to be listened to, and the right to be taken seriously*
- *I have the right to set my own priorities*
- *I have the right to change my mind*
- *I have the right to privacy*
- *I have the right to get professional help*
- *I have the right to be non-assertive*
- *I have the bodily right to walk away*

* * *

Our psyche might need one other thing to make it complete.

Many thinkers praise the effectiveness of prayer as divine grace, or in mundane terms, as a powerful suggestion to the subconscious. Yet several people do not pray. The reason could be that we are ignorant of how to pray or feel undeserving to pray genuinely.

Instead of feeling blessed, we may oscillate between fear and guilt when we attempt prayer. It is tough to ask for blessings or express gratitude when we doubt ourselves. On the other hand, our conditioning concerning worship may confuse loving and care for ourselves with selfishness or narcissism.

Sincerity and forgiveness are essential to pray or summon self-affirmations without a negative bias. We can never pray until we give ourselves the caring, kindness, and compassion we expect from the rest of the world.

We can lay every discouragement or struggle at the altar of existence and accept that our life is imperfect and does not need perfection. This is humility. We can forgive our trespasses and know we deserve the opportunity to improve ourselves. This is self-love.

Get over any awkwardness in your attempt at prayer. Caring prayer and loving affirmations work in ways that seem almost magical, whether you believe its power is divine, as in a God, or mundane, as in a suggestion to the subconscious. So forgive, persevere, and pray... sincerely.

* * *

This book ends here if you have already visited the Recovery Instruments (RIs) in the Appendix. However, if you are yet to see the RIs, do read and apply them as needed.

Life could be full of simple solutions to complex problems. But unfortunately, many think only complex solutions work because they feel their issues are insurmountable without complicated techniques.

I offered, in the book, some basic information, and ideas that have helped me. They can also help you develop your unique cognitive core.

The past, collective or individual, can no longer hold us back. Once you resolve to grow, all you go through, good and bad, will add to your experience.

The *five-minute promise* is a little technique to get you started, even if you cannot begin doing any RIs. You must promise yourself that you will devote five minutes to a real, achievable, and compelling task before deciding you cannot go on. So, give the job you pick your wholehearted attention for just five minutes. Let action precede motivation.

If the job does not grab you, and you feel apathetic, there is probably something physically wrong. You may need to bide your time or even seek professional help.

Go ahead and own your life on *your* terms. You can now accept and build, right here and right now, wherever you are and whatever you are. You will find that you and your existence are complete. You will not regret the past or fear the future when you are 'being (in the) here (and) now.'

THE BEGINNING?

APPENDIX:
RECOVERY INSTRUMENTS [RIs]

RI 1: FLYING ABOVE THE FLAK

The first RI to visit is 'Flying Above the Flak.' This provides a method to manage fear. Fear is usually the first impediment to the restoration of mental health. This RI would assist in dealing with critical and competitive environments that attempt to intimidate us or cause fear. Please apply the technique in this RI to free yourself from anxiety and fear. It will help you move closer to your own empowered, rational, and personal purpose.

Fear is a significant factor that prevents people from progressing. We may find it hard to start when we are timid about confronting challenges. No matter how much our cognitive understanding develops, historical dogma and impulses surface frequently.

There could be physical, mental, or emotional attempts to invade our space. As a result, we may end up feeling afraid. Instead of confronting such attempts proactively, fear can push us further into disturbing feelings.

This RI helps in remaining poised when afraid. One cannot banish fear, but we can manage it. A simple six-step process for fear-control based on Dr. Jerilyn Ross's original technique is included here[54]. Dr. Jerilyn

---

54 Ross, Jerilyn and Carter, Rosalynn: *Triumph Over Fear*; Bantam Books,1995

Ross (1946–2010) recommended these six steps in contextual therapy for overcoming anxiety.

While these steps were intended to treat extreme anxiety, they can also be applied to less severe manifestations. Coexisting with flawed learning within and around us may be gut-wrenching for some, even those not mentally afflicted. Please note: Dr. Ross's steps have been embellished with additional details in this book.

SIX STEPS TO MANAGE FEAR

Step 1. Expect, allow, and accept that fear will arise.

At the outset, do not be surprised when you feel fear. Fear is an emotion that needs to be managed, not conquered. Fear happens. We must accept this. The flawed historical basis is woven into our very beings as instinct; perhaps it is also in our genes (as fight or flight). There is no need to tackle fear by overcorrecting it with reckless disregard. As a first step, feeling fear, momentary or otherwise, is taken as a given.

Step 2. When fear comes, stop, wait, and refocus.

Some simple focus mechanisms are counting backward, in pre-determined even or uneven reductions (3, 6, 7, for example). For instance, count backward from 100, saying mentally 100…97…94…91… etc. A tougher alternative is to count upward, replacing multiples of five with "fizz" and seven with "buzz" (1, 2, 3, 4, fizz, 6, buzz, 8, 9, fizz…etc. For multiples of both, such as 35, use any one). You can also cope by feeling solid surfaces of different textures. For example, touch the arm of your chair, the fabric of your dress, the wall behind you, etc. Another method often used to overcome bad habits is wearing a rubber band around your wrist. You can snap the rubber band on the inside of your wrist until the fear starts subsiding. Such remedies can be continued until the anxiety becomes more manageable.

Step 3. Focus on doing manageable things in the present, and then build a sharper focus for more complex tasks.

This just means *move*. Don't be like a rabbit or a deer immobilized by a car's headlights. Move your muscles. Do some manageable things. Some manageable stuff could be listening or watching media clips, reading books, taking notes, drinking water, working out, making a sandwich, etc. Anything appropriate to the current situation, which the condition allows. Even chanting and pranayama can help. By doing this, you prevent yourself from sinking deeper into the fear. After this, you can go on to complex tasks following the next step.

Step 4. Rate your level of fear from zero to ten. Watch it go up and down.

This is a potent step for controlling fear. When you do this with concentration, the results will surprise you. Do this while responding to the anxiety, as in Step 3, when doing manageable tasks. Ask, *what is the level of fear I am feeling right now?* Zero is calmness and serenity; ten is the opposite— uncontrolled panic. Ten is the worst nightmare of what can happen to us or what we can do. Rate the level of fear on a scale of zero to ten and compare it with the situation.

As you measure it, you will feel your fear level changing. Never mind— keep measuring the level of fear. Now I am feeling a fear-level of six... now five...now it has gone up to seven...down to four...and so on. What this exercise does is remarkable. You will find that you are never out of control as far as 'fear' is concerned. The fear will go up and down as you keep giving it a measure, and you should soon be able to get a controllable fix. Be assured that it would never reach a ten on this scale.

Step 5. Function with fear. Appreciate your achievement.

One should practice continuing tasks while being afraid. The steps above should not require a break in activity. Bear the temporary discomfort and act. To the extent feasible, you need not suspend current tasks to engage in *fear management*. Instead, learn to feel good about the most minor tasks you achieve while feeling fear. You might have read a little, or you might have exercised, or you might have made yourself that sandwich you deserve... whatever. Just appreciate whatever little you can do. As your fears drop off, you will accomplish more.

Step 6. The last step. Expect, allow, and accept that fear will reappear.

This is step one said another way. Fear is not a feeling that one can leave behind. It is a natural mechanism. It must be managed and annulled repeatedly. Accept this as inevitable. Even your reaction to experiencing fear will change as you stop thinking, *why am I feeling afraid now?* Feeling fear is okay; you just need to manage it. You will not be surprised the next time you are scared. The six-step process can be set in motion as necessary.

Some of us would never need to use this tool. Nevertheless, it can be reassuring to know that one has it when confronting fear for any reason or even no reason. Apply the technique when you are afraid. You will see its effectiveness.

RI 2: THE ARCHIVED ANXIETY

The friends and foes in our history leave deep impressions on us. We are agitated and driven to some things because of harmful events in the past. Bad experiences may overly influence our decisions today. The impacts of such events on the psyche must be managed. This brings up the next RI to explore—*The Archived Anxiety*, a potent technique.

As explored early in the book, primal therapists first postulated that birth trauma affects us. 'A fractured primal integrity from a painful birth experience and unfulfilled primal needs may lead to a person's inability to live consciously and function fully without impairment[55].'

Moreover, the trauma we carry might have caused us to do some things early in our lives, which now are internal obstacles to our progress. For example, introversion, aloofness, shyness, and isolation often have

---

55 Stettbacher, Konrad J, *Making Sense of Suffering: The Healing Confrontation with Your Own Past*. New York, N.Y., U.S.A. Meridian, 1993

their roots in trauma in the womb or may be caused by pain early in life from factors like colic.

One of the best ways to remove these hurdles is healing confrontations with our own recollection of the past by writing out our history. The following is a summary of a method primal therapists have tested. It is recommended if you feel a need, but with caution. In primal therapy, *writing out history* is a precursor to professional help. Nonetheless, it has proved helpful to just sit at a computer and capture recollections of the past. Using pen and paper may be cumbersome but use whatever is comfortable. This writing might require a few hours over some days away from your usual routine. However, you can complete this process in a few sittings if you manage your time well.

The simplest way to achieve an enhanced level of personal integration is to write out one's history as an advocate of the child you were. I suggest that you write the record at least until fourteen years of age, though I found it helpful to continue it to later years.

Feel free to confront people in the past, perhaps in imaginary dialogues, while writing your history. Ask without false pride, as a child would. Feel free to justify the child's actions, who could have been carrying a historical load—such as the trauma of childbirth. Some recollections may be painful. If you have painful memories, it would be best to resolve them and not shy away from them. Be brave. Describe what you felt or feel now as you write. It just takes effort on your part. Try it and see.

To help you in the exercise, make two lists. First, a list of people you cannot forget because of how they influenced or affected you. Second, a list of events you cannot forget: Events that others caused and things you did that disturb you even today. With these lists ready, start writing your history in chronological order (as far as possible) and to the extent you remember. This means writing a telling commentary to protect yourself. Be your own lawyer. You were caught in the historical web and are unaccountable once you change.

In most cases, it is likely to be issues of communication that have caused your lapses. Something you left untold or failed to do, something misunderstood, or some abnormal behavior.

Also, look at the other side of the coin. Ask for forgiveness from others and seek restitution where it is needed. Learn to forgive others and yourself—all in your mind and writing. But, keep rewriting and enhancing until you reach a more comfortable present.

As you write this history, fortify the case for your old, immature self. The important thing about this exercise is not just the writing but the constant *rewriting.* You should write, rewrite, and make corrections and changes to your narration and the feelings captured. This does not mean we change facts. We just change our arguments, explanations, and reactions to our recollections.

Do this as often as required. This is why a computer is helpful. When we keep rereading and rewriting, it is not surprising to discover a sense of outrage, intimidation, anger, or sheepishness. But, as we progress, we find out a little more about ourselves every time we revisit and refine this history of ours. We can learn to forgive ourselves or others as we resolve long-standing conflicts. With some patience, at some point, you will feel released from the damaging thoughts, words, and events in your past.

This exercise might be challenging if your circumstances have not changed. What you want to forget may still be in front of you. But we can regain control by sitting down and confronting its genesis in the past. We may never realize how far-reaching the impact of our history is until we articulate its unfolding.

When we keep revisiting the articulation, we discover our point of view in it. We find that we deserve to be free. We may find we have to start over on some matters. If you have assimilated the concepts in this book so far, you will see that this starting over is nothing but a change in perspective. This perspective can be rooted in our personal purpose, measure for measure as we live.

I can state only my personal experience and the success of others in my immediate circle with history-writing. This is an initial step, under the controlled settings of primal therapy, in both the Janov and Stettbacher schools of Primal Therapy. Dr. Janov has stated the dangers of *self-primalling*. Nonetheless, the utility of history-writing as an insightful and strengthening exercise was evident.

I did experience some extreme emotions that were cathartic, but such feelings may not be tolerable for some. Hence, caution is advised. Please note that it is better to seek professional help if you encounter extreme uncontrollable emotions.

If some memories are harrowing, this is an indication that you have deep-set problems. Stop the effort at once. You should seek professional help. Remember that the idea is to benefit from the exercise and resolve issues, not regress. At the very least, you will come out with an incredibly sorted past or know if you need professional help. You win either way.

RI 3: FORGIVE TO FORGET

The next RI is for addressing those acts we regret now but justified cleverly in the past. So, to put the haunting memories to rest and become self-anchored, consider the next RI, *'Forgive to Forget.'*

All of us have collected some mental baggage. This sometimes blocks us from reasonableness and recovery. It might be as crucial for us to forget some things and allow them to fade as it is to forgive others and ourselves. It may be challenging to resolve some memories using only the 'history-writing' method.

These memories keep popping up periodically in our minds responding to some triggers, sometimes spontaneously. Science claims that there are *physical* traces of memory imprinted in our brains. Memory is dependent on four things:

- The intensity of the impression
- The number of times the event was repeated
- The interest in the event at the time
- The repetition of conditions like that in which the memory was formed.

It is possible to minimize the impact of memory and make it a non-issue eventually. As soon as an unpleasant memory arises, follow it with the conscious recall of another unrelated event, *even an unpleasant one,* comparable in intensity.

This seems a strange response, but it interferes with the earlier spontaneous memory. You can dwell on these and more such memories consciously, and this will cause a reduction in the intensity of *all* unpleasant memories.

When we do this repetitive flip-flopping among memories, we can come to the present, lessening the impact of negative recollection. The technique consciously uses two or more harsh events in the past, or also significant positive events, to interfere with the moment of unpleasant recall.

Turning highly disturbing memories into harmless forces is feasible with some practice. Try it. The memories of several unpleasant encounters could crop up randomly. Flag each one as a tool for helping to reduce the intensity of another.

When you think of one *faux pas,* voluntarily think of another, and then perhaps another. Keep flip-flopping among these. The key is to be conscious and recall the interfering memories by volition.

You must recognize it as a choice rather than a reaction to depression. This means you remain aware and in control throughout the process and do not feed a depressive state. Unusual as this may seem, it works. Try it.

You might want to also try a technique for those annoying memories of things you have done or missed—the minor gaffes, the irritants, the missed opportunities, etc. Memory interference is for the strong unpleasant memories, whereas this is for a milder class. The technique combines *history-writing* and *memory-interference*.

Carry a small flipbook with you. You can get flipbooks that fit in your wallet. First, write down a title for every annoying memory you can recall in the flipbook. Just one or two words for each specific memory by which you can identify them. Then, when a disturbing memory crops up randomly, open the flipbook and glance through your entire list quickly.

You can mobilize a relieving remission of any disturbing memory by just going through your list. Soon it will only be an item in your little book and not a struggle in your mind. Incidentally, you can keep up your list as you live your life. It is a good teacher.

One thing to remember from our explorations is that all this *had to happen*. Do not get into wallowing in the past, and be willing to take control from this point forward. It would be as essential to stop garnering bad memories as it is to defuse any past unpleasantness.

There are four things to do to prevent collecting bad memories, recommended by Geoffrey A. Dudley, a self-help author.[56]

1. Do not sleep with an unpleasant experience. Keep awake. Just put in the hours.
2. Do not allow the impression to settle. Instead, distract the mind with a movie, engaging book, or company. The more active we

---

56 Dudley, Geoffrey: *Double Your Learning Power*. Northhamptonshire: Thorsons Publishers, 1986.

are in the interval following the event, the more likely we will forget.

3. The more similar your activity following the unpleasant experience is to the prior experience, the easier it is to forget the unpleasant experience. This time, we have sufficient control to choose the subsequent activity and make it positive.

4. Trust time to heal.

RI 4: FIND GOLD IN OLD

We can refuse to degenerate and decay by finding new yardsticks for personal success in several ways. We explore this in the next RI, *'Find Gold in Old.'* There is scope for hope in every moment of life.

We often look at old age as something that happens to someone else. The finality of being in the 'old' bracket of life can be a surprise or yet another role we slip into comfortably. How we accept aging can change our lives. A lot has to do with managing our expectations for ourselves and the expectations others have of us.

Writing out our history and practicing memory-interference techniques could be necessary but may not be sufficient for some with a mental block. The block makes them feel they are too old to make changes. This chapter highlights a technique that can be applied by anybody who does not feel adequately detached, regardless of age. It is an easy-to-implement and widespread practice. It can help anyone mature emotionally.

* * *

Meditation is a beneficial technique for stability when aging. Note that the method is less important than the purpose. The purpose is to get a sense of detachment from the mind's constant chatter, to be an observer of our thoughts, and calm our thought stream. We are likely to become poised with a little step back, introspection, and a little contemplation.

Meditation has several techniques, and one of the best among them may be to observe breathing and the mind in tandem. Then, with some practice, we can keep the observer in us detached and calm any erratic thought stream. As an aid, we could also chant a non-associative, all-encompassing, symbolic representation of our choosing, such as OM[57] or Nam-Myo-Ho-Rengey-Kyo[58].

Focus on your mind when you chant. You may get random yet profound ideas, which typically get increasingly insightful when you meditate effectively. This will heighten your tendency to become involved with the mind and the thought stream. You can follow such thoughts to resolve any inconsistency in your insights or remove any conflict in your understanding.[59]

* * *

Being bold and attempting new techniques that pose no danger will be rewarding and aid in discovering the methods that work for you. Some have found remarkable growth with the practice of Tai Chi. Some others take up social or legal issues that were dear to their hearts but for which they never found the time. Others find it rewarding to share the knowledge gained from their experiences by writing, lecturing, or *satsang*[60]. Socialising and volunteering are also effective ways to keep the brain stimulated.

---

57 Om is the mystical sound that represents the source and entirety of creation for the Hindus. It is the basis for what can be called the 'gross' universe, the 'subtle' universe and the 'causal' universe.

58 This is the chant of the followers of Nichirin Buddhism. Myo- Ho-Rengey-Kyo is the name of the Lotus Sutra, in Japanese pronunciation of classical Chinese characters. The literal meaning of Nam-Myo-Ho-Rengey-Kyo is 'I devote myself to the Lotus Sutra.'

59 Some mental health researchers are of the opinion that meditation for recovering schizophrenia patients is not advisable. If you do not find meditating relaxing after trying it for a while, and if you feel a persistent anxiety when you attempt to meditate, do not adopt this technique.

60 A Sanskrit word for being in the company of an assembly of persons who listen to, talk about, and assimilate knowledge in search of the highest truth.

When speaking on a topic similar to the art of growing old gracefully, an educator and debater, N. B. Hardeman (1874–1965), said: 'I am too young to speak as one should on this subject.' He was over eighty at the time! Learning to be confident in your uniqueness, whatever your age, is feasible. Three key factors predicting solid mental function in old age are regular physical activity, a robust social support system, and a belief in one's ability to handle what life offers.

Judith Heyworth, M.D., the Medical Director and a geriatrician at Advocate Health Center, Sykes, offers this advice. 'As you grow older, you will face challenges and losses. However, my patients who seem to do the best mentally and physically are those who keep a positive attitude.' A good attitude helps you cope with life's vicissitudes. This is valid for people of all ages.

Medical authorities also say laughter is one of the best medicines for the elderly. You can always keep your sense of humor tuned up by surrounding yourself with pleasant and interesting people. Just act your age, and do not be afraid to laugh at yourself even when someone else is around.

* * *

Just a few methods or platitudes cannot alleviate the challenge of old age. As the saying goes, 'Old age is not for sissies.' Fully use the information and techniques in the book. Then, go out and grab life in whatever capacity you can. You will get to feel fuller and more confident as you age.... You can be sure the innately progressive core in you will see you through safely all your life.

RI 5: BEGINNING TO START OVER

This next RI looks at grief and heartbreak. How can we talk of personal purpose when suffering the loss of a loved one? The Recovery Instruments for handling grief and heartbreak that follow are only a token of thought.

No one can give you a shortcut when it comes to loss. No book can ever replace what you have lost. You could find books that may help, but what you learn from this ultimate challenge is yours and yours alone. So, treat the little learnings and the earth-shaking ones preciously.

* * *

GRIEF: Grief is an issue we should let slip into the past. Intellectual acceptance that it cannot be any other way may need to precede emotional reconciliation. It is best to remember the difference we explored between destiny and fate.

Death is an aspect of fate, not destiny. Understanding death, therefore, is a part of assimilating and accepting life[61]. Life is as much a mystery as death. Hence, despite its poetic tone, we should acknowledge the death of others we have outlived in the same manner we joyfully accepted their living.

Given its mystery, it is inevitable that solace, if sought, is found only in theology. The best alternative to theological explanations I have come across is from a child about six years old. This child rationalized death with originality. He said, 'People die to make room for babies (!).'

But then, how can we manage the loss if it is the death of a child? Here is where theology can help. Hinduism and Buddhism suggest that early death occurs when an advanced soul reincarnates. When a soul close to freedom from the cycle of birth and rebirth is born, it lives in the world for a brief period. It has a tiny amount of *karma* to work out, and this short life span allows it to do so. Other religions suggest that God loved the soul of the departed so much that he could not wait to have them back, so he called them back early.

When one loses someone dear to the ultimate deadline, it is an unparalleled lesson in personal growth. We must learn to appreciate

------

61 As further reading, McWilliams, Peter, and Harold Bloomfield: *How to Survive the Loss of a Love*. Prelude Press, 1993.

good memories and keep building as many good new ones as we can, as quickly as we can. We need to work out our grief and not let it overwhelm us.

Try to see that you have outlived the departed as a blessing. You may have saved the departed extreme pain had you preceded them. Their death was brought about by the compassion of an invisible hand, protecting them from pain and suffering had they lived.

We must allow grief to work itself out in a personally meaningful way. A method like writing out one's history can help overcome grief. We can sometimes assuage our grieving by writing a letter to the departed. Write in a personal diary or on a computer, and pour the anger, love, frustration, and other feelings induced by the loss into it.

You could find other meaningful ways to help deal with the loss. Examples are, carrying out an activity dear to the person lost as homage or closing out any vision they would have liked to make a reality. Only look forward once you have done this letter-writing and/or homage.

Table 3. STATEMENTS TO HELP BUILD A LETTER TO THE DEPARTED

- I admire you because...
- I should have done with you <all this>...
- If I meet you again, I will...
- I miss you because...
- I should have told you...
- I am sorry for...
- I dedicate to you <all this>

You must overcome defeatist urges, such as the anger or temporary masochism that grief may bring. The departed would want you to be happy. The departed would want to save you your pain. The departed would want you to move on. Cherish the memories you have of them.

* * *

HEARTBREAK: You could have felt a pain like grief—heartbreak. We generally experience heartbreak when we are young. Youthfulness need not be in years but in emotional maturity. The 'object of our affection' often becomes perfect to us, whatever the footing on which the relationship started. We could have started thinking, *this is the best thing that ever happened to me*, or maybe *let's see how it goes*, or even *this will do for now*. The heart invariably idealizes what it loves. Heartbreak is almost inevitable when we idealize and then lose the person.

One way to overcome heartbreak is to discover a relationship's 'opportunity cost.' This means finding the things you are now free to do that you could not do before. One must think *release* rather than *loss*. An examination of one's life, sometime after the heartbreak, would give reasons, however obscure, for a life without the lost person.

Recognize that love is more than a focus between you and another. Love is more extensive than you and me, so we cannot conclude we have a monopoly and disregard everyone else. On the contrary, to have loved and lost is usually a foundation to love better than ever.

One of the best preventions for heartbreak is not idealizing but broadening our perspective. But, first, we need to acknowledge that no one or no relationship can be eternally or constantly perfect and need not be so to qualify as successful.

The past is not immaculate, and the future is always promising without being perfect. Move on.

* * *

Peter McWilliams (1949–2000) and Dr. Harold Bloomfield provide the following pointers in their book, Overcoming the Loss of a Love (Table 4 - *Points to Help Us Move On*). These can help tackle the emotional weight of parting from another. These can be applied to parting from another while alive (heartbreak) and the permanent parting by death (grief).

TABLE 4. Points to Help Us Move On

- To forgive does not just mean to pardon. It means to let go.
- Jesus, probably the greatest teacher of forgiveness in history [Forgive them, Father, for they know not what they do], used the Aramaic word *shaw*. Shaw means, 'to untie.'
- If you are tied to a rock that is pulling you down in the water, all you must do is forgive it (untie it) and swim toward the light.
- When you forgive the past, you untie yourself from the past, and you are free.
- To forgive also means to be for (in favor of) giving (to deliver a gift). When you forgive, you affirm that you are in favor of giving.
- To whom do you give? Another? Sometimes. Yourself? Always. When you release another to go their way, you free yourself to do the same. The process of giving oneself this gift of freedom is forgiveness
- The waiting may be difficult, but one can trust time to heal. Time will cradle you in its natural cycle. It is benevolent even as it is demanding. Often, life will provide strength, even as it tests it. Look forward... Look outward... Reach out, and you will be pleasantly surprised at how living helps. Life lives. Take courage.

RI 6: THE LAST ERROR

You have read the discussions and techniques so far, but there could still be one hurdle—habitual negative thoughts. The last RI to visit is *The Last Error*. This RI will help you handle disturbing and unhelpful thinking. Despite discovering your personal purpose, you may have such thoughts just out of habit.

Why do you have disturbing thoughts, although you understand there is no need to be disturbed? First, step back from troubling thoughts as a precursor to emotional maturity. Then, you can check to see if you are committing an error in your thinking[62].

The last error is an error in thinking, continuing to think in the same manner as in the past, despite having progressive ideas. Despite our understanding, deep-set discouraging beliefs may keep replaying in our minds. To handle these, become conscious of the type of error in your thinking.

You can flag any unhelpful or disturbing thought into one of the following ten types and discard or challenge it. Actively classifying the thought into the types below will help free you from negativity.

ARE YOU...

1. **Predicting the future?** The future is always yet to happen. Remember the fate-destiny distinction. Do not predict the future by indulging in negative imaging. You have control over how you meet what you meet. Affirm to yourself when you face difficulties that you can have control and that you deserve 'grace.'

2. **Jumping to conclusions?** So what if a person you know did not say hello when you saw him or her in public? There may have been a million things going through the person's mind. Do not jump to conclusions based on superficial observations. You cannot conclude negatively from an event that could be random. Do not overdo it in your imagination.

---

62 This 'last mile' is based on the path-breaking work of Dr Aaron Beck. Dr Beck is professor emeritus in the department of psychiatry at the University of Pennsylvania. He is regarded as the father of cognitive therapy, and his pioneering theories are widely used in the treatment of clinical depression. This is a short-list of some ideas derived from his work, but with some embellishments. I have attempted, to the best of my ability, not to underplay or misconstrue Dr Beck's original work. I apologize for any shortfall in articulation and take full responsibility for any errors.

3. **Over-generalizing?** Just because something happened in a particular way in the past, does not mean it will happen the same way now. Do not make the mistake of discerning a negative pattern when there is none. Give it a rest.

4. **Focusing on the negative?** Every dark cloud has a silver lining. Learn to recognize it. Every story has two sides. Do not just read one. Look for positive facts if you do not want to feel miserable. Some events tend to drag us down, but that is temporary. Take control and absorb what is constructive and can be helpful to you.

5. **Focusing on Weakness?** Okay, so you have some weaknesses. However, do not forget your strengths. Cast away that focus on your liabilities. Cannot concentrate now? No sweat! You'll get it right eventually. You don't have a very disciplined or organized schedule. Not a problem! You need to do this spontaneously. You *have* a purpose and can discover the ability to do just what you are supposed to do. Do not dwell on your weaknesses.

6. **Thinking in extremes?** Life is not black and white but shades of grey. It is not all good or bad, but a mix of both. Become conscious of thinking in extremes. See the grey instead of just black and white. There are degrees of good and bad in every situation, every person, and every incident. It is not simply good *or* bad, even if it might seem so at that moment. There is no need to get totally euphoric or completely dismayed.

7. **Expecting perfection?** If you have been expecting perfection from yourself, it is time to wake up. A perfect 10 is an Olympic score. A few of us *are* equipped to get a perfect score in figure skating. However, all of us, including our Olympian champions, need not apply such a measure to everyday life. Instead, let the facts of your effort speak.

   If your intent is correct, you can accept the result and commit to getting better. On some issues, you may even recognize a point of diminishing returns... where the effort you need to put in outweighs the improvement you can make.

8. **Self-blaming?** If things go wrong, do not take all the blame. Several things contribute to success and failure. If you think you alone are to blame, it is time to flag that thought. Remember the 'Uncertainty' model and Karma. Many factors shape the results. Disconnect from any masochistic need that prompts you to punish yourself.

9. **Reasoning emotionally?** Do not think you know what others feel just because of your feelings. Do not assume others have a hotline to your emotions. You think in private. Nobody caught that slight tremor in your voice during your last stage performance. Do not assume that others' actions result from your internal emotions.

10. **Thinking about or blaming the past?** Focus on the present. The past is where it belongs. It does not matter at what stage in life you are or how deep you are into an interaction. Your worries about the past and its impact can be converted into learning. MOVE ON. If you are alive, there is a tomorrow. Your mission is not complete. If you have difficulty disengaging from the past, try the history-writing and memory-interference techniques explored earlier.

You should challenge every disturbing thought that comes into your mind. Practice stepping back and categorizing problematic or unhelpful thoughts into the 10 types discussed.

The very act of doing this is essential. This act is a progressive step that interrupts the harmful flow. Classifying the errors in thinking is a simple yet effective technique.

You would find it easier to apply the technique by carrying a small card with the titles of these ten points. Then, when you feel disturbed, fish out the card and weigh any anxious thoughts against the list. After some practice, you can refocus your thoughts and manage the mind's chatter. With some effort, you will find you can tame a wild mind. You will soon transform yourself into a confident thinker.

* * *

In closing, if you habitually feel uneasy or in a bind, discount it by recollecting some things you find fulfilling or some things good about yourself. Think of a few uplifting things like a pet welcoming you home, the laughter of an infant, or even 'raindrops on roses and whiskers on kittens.[63]'

When you think you are undeserving, say to yourself, 'I deserve what life has to offer me.' When you feel your inner calm disturbed, say to yourself, 'Relax, this will also pass.' Finally, when someone knocks down your work with destructive criticism, say, 'I am getting better and better each day.'

There are three kinds of self-assurances you can give yourself that should help to counter discouraging thinking.

1. I believe in myself (in my skills, temperament, etc.)
2. I deserve the good things (leisure, compliments, etc.)
3. I am improving every day (growing, getting wiser, etc.)

Say these things and their variants to yourself as if you do not have a care in the world. A constructive change will then happen steadily. How you see yourself, how people see you, and your actions will take on an aura of excellence. The change will occur in 'real time' as you learn to keep being proactive. Soon you will be poised, even in severely challenging situations.

* * *

The last of the Recovery Instruments or heuristics have been shared. You can build the ability to mitigate any fringe symptoms and negativity by practicing the RIs.

Don't attach any stigma to reaching out. It is in you to get real, build confidently and look ahead. It is never ever too late. Trust life, and life will trust you. So, get started with being here now!

---

63 From the song *"Favorite Things"* in the classic film *Sound of Music* (1965)

EPILOGUE

The book assumes that medication can work across a broad spectrum of those afflicted. For as many patients for whom medication works, there is an equal, if not greater, a number for whom it doesn't.

Therefore, recognizing the perspective that one is a survivor and not a victim is what helps, rather than just medication. There is a case to see symptoms, like hallucinations and delusions, as consequences of early or prenatal trauma to the self and that they are not caused by chemical imbalances alone.

Our psyche is trying to resolve itself by presenting such manifestations. If so, our ability to work collaboratively with these manifestations, instead of feeling victimized, will eventually help us.

I reproduce the following tenets of the Hearing Voices Movement, a movement devoted to demystifying and removing the stigma attached to such symptoms.

- Hearing voices is a common human experience that is not a symptom of illness, although it can cause distress.
- Distressing voices can be metaphors for problems in the hearer's life.
- The voices can be resolved by addressing the underlying emotions and conflicts they represent.

These are quoted from Eleanor Longden's e-book. *Learning from the Voices in My Head* (TED Books) (Kindle Locations 1022-1024). TED

Conferences. Kindle Edition. She provides helpful information and tips on confronting, coping, and collaborating with such manifestations.

While not free of problems, all of us can focus on our blessings. We can accept that we cannot change what we cannot influence and drive what we *can* control with gusto.

Our security is unaffected by possessions and is based on confidence in our abilities. We understand there will be enough air to last us until our last breath and have faith that the rest will also be there.

Better we have faith in a universal force, that something guides us. This belief is constructive and reflects confidence. Progressive things happen. If our beliefs are destructive or defeatist, negative emotions like fear, guilt, aggression, and resentment will hold their sway.

But, if we take small steps towards becoming proactive and confident consistently, we change gradually at the core of our beings. We attract the forces that keep making us better. Personal yet purposeful direction has a self-multiplying effect.

You grow inexorably with time; hence you surely will progress. If we go about the business of life, focusing on bettering our state of mind every day, we evolve. This evolution is a natural consequence of time and does not contradict the species' journey.

To be human is to care. Care for *yourself* and others. To care is the starting point of responsible living. We then travel through the understanding of many paradigms, none of which may ever be or *needs* to be complete.

There will always be gaps. It is meant to be this way. This is the way the cosmos maintains our *independent interdependence*. If we desire an ultimate goal and grace, we may need to understand that we already have it.

As you move in time, place all that has happened behind. All that has occurred can be a foundation for new ventures from this point forward.

You have strengthened the foundations themselves, whatever their state. Now build boldly. Live out the rest of your life, whatever the number of days (or minutes!), with caring and without fear or malice.

Just choose, discover, and care to be the *human* you are, and all that could be 'God' will take care of the rest.

MORE HELP?

You can get in touch with me at the following website. I will receive your request and respond as quickly as possible.

https://beingherenow.in

Wish you wellness,

Ganesh N Rajan

A LITTLE BIT OF HISTORY AND A LOT OF THANK YOUS

My first child was born in 1994. The doctor assured my wife and me that he was normal. But you know how it is with first-time parents. My questions about what could go wrong would not stop.

The doctor then began interrogating me about my health and my spouse's. In retrospect, the doctor was probably trying to dismiss me because her professional opinion that everything was okay did not stop me.

When I mentioned schizophrenia, she said, though not fully validated, there is a slightly increased chance of the offspring of afflicted persons developing schizophrenia. Everyone has a random chance of one percent, and my son, *perhaps* a tiny fraction more.

Right then, despite the minuscule chance of its occurrence, I decided that I must educate my son (and subsequently, daughter) on this condition.

I searched for a book that would explain what I had experienced. I wanted a book that included lessons for the *normal*. Unfortunately, I couldn't find any [at that time]. I, therefore, did the next best thing and wrote some notes for my children to read. The book you have just read is a metamorphosis of those notes over two decades.

Many people helped develop this book, and I appreciate and thank them. Firstly, three people in my immature past for showing me how twisted reality can be and who will remain anonymous in deference to the fact that all of us have moved on. Secondly, Swami Dayanandaji, for leading me to the ideas which helped me to a new beginning.

Finally, for constructive and corrective inputs or assistance in the book taking its final shape and reaching you, the following, in chronological order of their help: Susan (Gita), Khandadi, Mr. Seshan, Shanker, (Late) Mr. Ganapathy, Ramnarayan, Gayathri, Yathiraj, Ranjini, Dr. Tharoor, Geetha, (Late) Shivalingappa, Jo (Jyothi), (Late)

Mrs. Shastri, Dr. Mohan, Dr. Samuel, Vatsala, Arun, Col. Ajay, Ankush, Sanjana, Mr. Bhanu, Suresh, Arvind, Kishore, Anand, Mr. Jayaraman, Jaishanker, Tommy (Prakash), Gautam, Prita, Sanghamitra, Shrutika, Sudha, Krishna Kumar, Vipin, and Rahul.

Thank you, Gopi, Yamini, and Kush, for helping with the second edition. A very special thank you to Sangeetha Chengappa for her invaluable feedback.

And, of course, I thank you, my reader! I hope this book has helped you to rejoice in yourself... enduringly—GNR

www.ingramcontent.com/pod-product-compliance
Lightning Source LLC
Chambersburg PA
CBHW021152160726
47994CB00001B/169